# A PHILOSOPHY OF LUXURY

"Luxury has a bad reputation, built on marble and gold, boutique shopping and penthouse suites. This award-winning book, finally available in English, forces us to rethink all of that. Wiesing separates luxury from vulgar displays of wealth and power. Instead, he shows that it is an important aesthetic experience, available to all of us. Erudite, accessible, and beautifully translated, *Luxury* promises to become a classic of philosophical aesthetics."

– John V. Kulvicki, Dartmouth College, USA

In this thought-provoking book Lambert Wiesing asks simply: What is luxury? Drawing on a fascinating range of examples, he argues that luxury is an aesthetic experience. Unlike experience gained via the senses, such as seeing, hearing or tasting, he argues that luxury is achieved by possessing something – an aspect of philosophy that has been largely neglected. As such, luxury becomes a gesture of individual defiance and a refusal to conform to social expectations of restraint. An increasingly rational and goal-oriented ethos in society makes the appeal of luxury grow even stronger.

Drawing on the ideas of philosophers such as Immanuel Kant, Friedrich Schiller, Martin Heidegger and the novelist Ernst Jünger, as well as sociologists such as Thorstein Veblen and Theodor Adorno, *A Philosophy of Luxury* will be of great interest to those in philosophy, art, cultural studies and literature as well as sociology.

**Translated by Nancy Ann Roth**

**Lambert Wiesing** is Chair of Image Theory and Phenomenology at Friedrich Schiller University, Jena, Germany. His books include *Artificial Presence: Philosophical Studies in Image Theory* (2009) and *The Philosophy of Perception: Phenomenology and Image Theory* (2014).

# A PHILOSOPHY OF ECOLOGY

# A PHILOSOPHY OF LUXURY

*Lambert Wiesing*

*Translated by Nancy Ann Roth*

LONDON AND NEW YORK

This edition published 2019
by Routledge
2 Park Square, Milton Park, Abingdon, Oxon OX14 4RN

and by Routledge
52 Vanderbilt Avenue, New York, NY 10017

*Routledge is an imprint of the Taylor & Francis Group, an informa business*

First published in German as *Luxus* by Suhrkamp Verlag AG, 2015

English Translation © 2019, Routledge
Foreword © 2019, Lambert Wiesing

All rights reserved. No part of this book may be reprinted or
reproduced or utilised in any form or by any electronic,
mechanical, or other means, now known or hereafter invented,
including photocopying and recording, or in any information
storage or retrieval system, without permission in writing from
the publishers.

*Trademark notice*: Product or corporate names may be
trademarks or registered trademarks, and are used only for
identification and explanation without intent to infringe.

*British Library Cataloguing-in-Publication Data*
A catalogue record for this book is available from the British Library

*Library of Congress Cataloging-in-Publication Data*
Names: Wiesing, Lambert, author.
Title: A philosophy of luxury / Lambert Wiesing ; translated by
Nancy Ann Roth.
Other titles: Luxus. English
Description: 1 [edition]. | New York : Routledge, 2019. |
Includes bibliographical references and index.
Identifiers: LCCN 2019004473| ISBN 9780367138400
(hardback : alk. paper) | ISBN 9780367138417 (pbk. : alk. paper) |
ISBN 9780429028816 (e-book)
Subjects: LCSH: Luxury. | Aesthetics.
Classification: LCC BJ1535.L9 W5413 2019 | DDC 128/.4–dc23
LC record available at https://lccn.loc.gov/2019004473

ISBN: 978-0-367-13840-0 (hbk)
ISBN: 978-0-367-13841-7 (pbk)
ISBN: 978-0-429-02881-6 (ebk)

Typeset in Bembo
by Swales & Willis, Exeter, Devon, UK

Printed in the United Kingdom
by Henry Ling Limited

# CONTENTS

| | | |
|---|---|---|
| *Foreword to the English edition* | | *vi* |
| Introduction | | 1 |

**PART I**
**Play, then war, anxiety and drugs—and now, luxury 11**

| 1 | Anthropology and the idea of self-experience | 13 |
|---|---|---|
| 2 | Aesthetics and the search for moments of self-experience | 33 |

**PART II**
**Luxury: the Dadaism of possession**     **51**

| 3 | The judgment of luxury | 53 |
|---|---|---|
| 4 | Luxury: a special aesthetic experience | 85 |
| 5 | Why luxury? | 132 |

| | |
|---|---|
| *Detailed table of contents* | *161* |
| *Bibliography* | *163* |
| *Index* | *169* |

# FOREWORD TO THE ENGLISH EDITION

For years before actually beginning to work, I had entertained a vague idea about writing a book on luxury. For quite a long time I could not understand why the topic had received practically no attention at all in philosophy. It may be that this book is the first monograph specifically focused on luxury in either German or English. Still, it took a push from outside to really engage with what was, for me, new terrain. This push came when I was a Visiting Professor at Oxford University in Trinity term 2013. Much to my surprise, the unique, previously unfamiliar character of this university, as I got to know it in St Edmund Hall, made me associate education with luxury as much as luxury with education, and this for a simple reason: Luxury and education are available only to those who partially resist the wild expansion of utilitarian thinking and instrumental reason in our time. This is, in any case, how I arrived at the idea of treating luxury as an anthropological phenomenon, more exactly as a phenomenon of liberation and defiance that matters to people, and I decided to give a detailed description of luxury from this perspective.

As I was working on the book in the two years that followed, I received the most diverse kinds of encouragement and suggestions, criticisms and cautions. Sometimes even a little tip from a colleague regarding a special question was helpful, sometimes it was in-depth commentary on earlier drafts of the whole text. Whatever kind of support it may have been, I would like to express my heartfelt thanks

Foreword to the English edition  **vii**

to: Stefan Matuschek, Manfred Sommer, Silke Müller, Jens Bonnemann, Thomas Zingelmann, Wolfgang Ullrich, Thomas Jahn, Eva Gilmer, Ludger Sandknop, Friedrich Lauschke, Stephan Günzel, Katja Vollenberg, Bianca Weiß, Jason Gaiger, Hartmut Rosa, Nico Brömßer, Katerina Deligiorghi, Sascha Prescher, Klaus Vieweg, Andrea Seyfarth, Juliane Köster and Eckhard Meineke.

Happily, I can report that since it appeared in German in 2015, the book has been reviewed widely and discussed extensively. I have a sense of acknowledgment in noting that luxury has become a central issue in philosophy, and more particularly in an aesthetics of possession—a highly current issue, especially in light of ongoing social developments. It seemed clear that the book should be translated into English. I received substantial support from colleagues and friends in planning the project, for which I would like to thank John Armitage und John Kulvicki. My thanks, too, to two anonymous reviewers at Routledge for their helpful thoughts and comments, and to Michael Jenewein for his help with the translation.

But my greatest thanks must certainly go to Nancy Ann Roth for her exceptionally successful translation. I am impressed with how sensitively and accurately Nancy manages to translate fine philosophical distinctions into reliably graceful English.

**Amelsbüren, January 2019, L.W.**

# INTRODUCTION

David Hume published the essay "Of Luxury" in 1752. To look at it today is to get a disconcerting feeling that not much has changed since then! The text reads as if it had just been written recently. This is particularly the case for the main assertions. Hume makes it clear—there are just two opinions that shape thinking about luxury:

> While men of libertarian principles bestow praise even on vicious luxury and represent it as highly advantageous to society, men of strenuous morals blame even the most innocent luxury and represent it as the source of all the corruptions, disorders, and factions, incident to civil government.[1]

It is in this respect that the situation has hardly changed—although today we would not be speaking only of men. Nor is it very remarkable, for it must be said, the literature on luxury is modest. It is not central to contemporary research in the humanities, and the few relevant contributions there are oscillate back and forth, incessantly and inflexibly—between censure and glorification. It is still the case today: No matter where one looks, whether in philosophy, in sociology, in economics, in theology or even in the broad field of self-help literature, for every walk of life, there is hardly anything beyond variations of the two classic views. It seems as if some *tertium non datur* is in effect: Luxury is either treated as a problem—if not condemned outright—on social and moral grounds, as

**2** Introduction

Jean-Jacques Rousseau put it in *Emile* of 1762: "This is how luxury and bad taste become inseparable. Wherever taste is expensive, it is false"[2] or luxury is defended, if not glorified outright, on economic and political grounds, always returning to the argument familiar from Bernard Mandeville's famous work of 1714, *The Fable of the Bees*: "The Root of evil Avarice, That damn'd ill-natur'd baneful Vice, was slave to Prodigality, That Noble Sin; whilst Luxury Employ'd a Million of the Poor."[3] In short, from looking over the literature on luxury over the last 300 years, one could diagnose an "ambivalence toward excess in the modern period," as is aptly suggested in the subtitle of Christine Weder and Maximilian Bergengruen's 2011 anthology *Luxus*.[4]

This is not to cast doubt on the value of discussing the benefits and disadvantages of luxury. Yet it may be equally uncontroversial that for just such a discussion it would be advantageous to know what luxury actually is. We would like to know, after all, what is being praised and condemned. It really is a serious problem, for if we consider the discussion of luxury's economic and moral value—or the absence of value—from this point of view, we must be prepared for disappointment. Normally, it is simply assumed that everyone knows what luxury is. If it is defined at all, then it is only in passing in a few sentences, or in a concise dictionary definition such as the one found in the work by luxury's great defender, Werner Sombart: "Luxury is any expenditure that exceeds necessity."[5] Apologists, as well as critics, work with an easy definition of luxury, usually associating it with excess and prodigality, prestige objects or status symbols, with wealth and comfort, with freeloading and conspicuous consumption, lumping expensive bric-a-brac and pretentious ostentation together. The tenor of the treatment of luxury in the literature is consistent: It is frequently evaluated, but rarely described. The situation is thoroughly familiar from other discussions. At least there is a close correspondence between the forms of inquiry and interests that have almost always determined the way luxury has been studied and those that shape the discussion of, for example, atomic energy. Here, too, the dominant questions are: Is atomic energy sinful, necessary, antisocial, inevitable, irresponsible or imprudent? Would we rather live in a world with or without atomic energy? The same questions guide reflections on luxury: Is luxury sinful, necessary, antisocial, inevitable, irresponsible or imprudent? Does luxury make human life better or worse? Would we rather live in a world with or without luxury?

Introduction **3**

This very comparison with atomic energy, although perhaps unexpected, can show how odd the situation is for the discussion of luxury. For what is easy with atomic energy is difficult with luxury. At least the question "What is atomic energy?" has a clear answer, very different from the question "What is luxury?" If we would like to know what a nuclear reactor is and how it works, we turn to physicists and engineers. If there is disagreement about whether atomic energy is a boon or a threat to a modern society, we know what we are arguing about. And, still more importantly, those in dispute can be sure that they have different views of the same object. Not even that is the case for the controversy about luxury.

It is, in fact, inexplicable and incomprehensible. The question "What is luxury?" is not a field of systematic research in the humanities. Compare this topic with other social, aesthetic and cultural phenomena. How much theoretical and scientific effort is invested in answering the question "What is beauty?" for example? Or, "What is justice?" Hardly anyone would be content with a dictionary definition in answer to these questions. There are long-standing, intensive debates about the meanings of these concepts. That is, there is a concern with understanding the intension of the concepts, or to say it in another way: What do we know when we know that something is beautiful or that it is just? In comparison with this, we must emphasize that there is no study of luxury that even comes close to this standard—at least not in the sense of a number of people currently working systematically on the problem of what is meaningfully intended by the concept of luxury. The field rather continues to consist of isolated suggestions.[6] We are very far from a complex, differentiated research field such as we obviously find for concepts of, say, beauty and also justice. Opinions diverge on the question of whether luxury is to be judged good or bad. But with respect to the question of the criteria that make it possible for something to be a luxury in the first place, there has been no discussion, to say nothing of any articulation of differing philosophical positions that would understand the concept and with it the relevant criteria in entirely different ways. The questions at hand are: What must be the case for an object to be rightly called a *luxury*? What does one know about something when one knows that it is a luxury? In the process, we should not overlook the excellent historical contributions that carefully reconstruct details of the way the controversy over luxury developed. As already mentioned, the ambivalence of luxury

**4** Introduction

in the modern period—at once the object of contempt and the object of glorification—has been and is thoroughly researched.[7] But as helpful and necessary as historical knowledge is, it cannot replace systematic work toward a meaningful understanding of luxury.

This book is neither an apology for nor a criticism of luxury; there will be no judgment of its existence. The goal of the work is rather to answer the question "What is luxury?" This is to be done solely by means of a description of luxury, and more specifically by means of a resolutely phenomenological description. The phenomenological perspective was chosen because it suits the topic, and this for a simple reason: The question "What is luxury?" can be answered neither scientifically nor in any other way that refers to objective, material facts about luxury goods. You can ask a jeweller to examine a necklace to see whether it is made of genuine gold—but not to see whether it is genuine luxury. You cannot tell from looking at something whether it is a luxury, for it may be for one person and not for another. But if this is the case, it raises the question "Why isn't everything a luxury?" How can it be that calling something a luxury is not perfectly arbitrary? If not its material qualities, what is it that determines whether something has the status of a luxury? Here is a suggestion for resolving these problems. It goes: Something becomes a luxury by being experienced by a person in a particular way. So luxury is always something for someone—and more specifically for someone whose possession of that something is bound up with a particular kind of experience. The approach to the description of luxury just suggested has been known in aesthetics for a long time. For it is also the case that beauty—at least if we hold to Immanuel Kant's understanding of it—does not depend for its existence on the material qualities of something, but rather on the particular experience of its receiver. This furnishes the basic methodological idea of the argumentation that follows: Luxury is no more explicable by means of ontological qualities than beauty is; something is beautiful and something is a luxury on the basis of its mental effect on people—and this is the reason the phenomenological perspective fits so well. A luxury is a phenomenon in the specifically phenomenological sense of the word: A something that is *for* someone. Nuclear power stations can be described either scientifically or phenomenologically, luxury only phenomenologically. For luxury is nothing other than a phenomenon. In other words: Without people there would be no luxury. If human

Introduction **5**

beings disappeared from the world, luxury, too, would cease to exist. But nuclear reactors would still be there, for their existence is not bound to human experience. This is the reason the description of luxury presents a truly classic phenomenological task, namely the determination of what in particular characterizes the way luxury goods are given. That is the subject of this book: The search for principles of the way something must be experienced in order for it to be a luxury for someone. The thesis of this book goes: This experience which constitutes luxury in the world of human beings is a properly aesthetic experience.

It is not unlikely that this thesis on luxury as an aesthetic experience will irritate, if not actually aggravate, some readers. This may arise from a simple misunderstanding, but may also be based on a clear difference of opinion. The simple, if annoying, misunderstanding arises when the description of luxury is thought to be extolling something aesthetically noteworthy about ostentation, conspicuous consumption and exaggerated wealth. In order to avert this misunderstanding from the start, let it be said here as clearly as possible, that these frequently unsympathetic expressions of a not infrequently naïve self-aggrandizement by means of a phenomenological description of luxury will not be ennobled or in any way glossed over. The opposite is the case: By thinking of luxury as a form of *aesthetic self-awareness*, doubt arises about whether the *symbolic self-expression* through ostentation can be called luxury at all. Luxury and ostentation are treated as two phenomena with categorically different foundations—and this in particular supports the belief that the question "What is luxury?" cannot be answered using the methods of a theory of symbols. For by fulfilling a symbolic function for someone, for example by putting the owner's purchasing power on display, an object may become a mark of ostentation or of prestige, but not luxury. Being luxury—and this is the main idea of this book—is bound up with a specific aesthetic experience on the part of the owner.

The next two points are meant to position the following description of luxury with respect to the critical tradition of Theodor W. Adorno. In 1941, in a short, little-noticed yet enormously rigorous critique of the sociologist Thorstein Veblen's critique of luxury, Adorno put forward the idea that substantially shaped the phenomenological description of luxury attempted here: Namely the idea, first, of strictly,

**6** Introduction

categorically distinguishing luxury from "meaningless ostentatious display,"[8] so as, second, to think of it instead as a special moment of "emancipation from the realm of utility."[9] One can actually say, according to Adorno, a phenomenology of luxury has the task of showing, through description of the phenomenon itself, that the experience of luxury—like the experience of art, to which both he and most other aestheticians devote far more attention—belongs to the basic possibilities for an autonomous subject to "escape the slavery of utility."[10] It may be immediately clear, as well as in keeping with the sense of Adorno's statement, that such a phenomenon of luxury is being credited with an aesthetic, ultimately anthropological relevance that contradicts the notions of the *Bildungsbürgertum* [educated middle class]. For the thesis goes: The subject with a mind of his own, who does not want to be completely co-opted by a functional society, is present in, among other things, luxury.

Still, it is not only when the difference between luxury and ostentation is overlooked that the description of luxury as an aesthetic experience *sui generis* provokes irritation; it also runs into an explicit, overt rejection by representatives of traditional reception aesthetics. From the standpoint of the well-educated middle class, aesthetic experience necessarily arises from an artistic attitude of disinterestedness—which in this respect coincides exactly with Kant's view; in conventional aesthetics, a recipient is understood to be a contemplative viewer. But this ideal of the receiver cannot be reconciled with the thesis of luxury as a form of aesthetic experience. On the contrary: This thesis casts doubt on the foundation of an aesthetic in which only mental, intentional objects are suitable for aesthetic experiences, and the possession of an aesthetic object plays no part. In keeping with the basic assumption that continues to shape reception aesthetics, an aesthetic experience is one that changes one's own perception: Seeing, hearing, feeling, even smelling—but not possessing. Possession is simply not there. Even if we think of all the forms of sensual perception, even if we include fantasizing and reading, the wide spectrum of possible forms of aesthetic experience is unnecessarily narrowed and reduced as long as aesthetic experience is thought to be exclusively a *special experience of perception*. Human beings don't experience the world through perception alone, after all, and do not depend exclusively on perception for their experience of the world. The phenomenology of luxury makes an effort to

Introduction **7**

expose possession as a mental condition that has a capacity to be modified into a genuine aesthetic experience of autonomy. Possessing something brings a subject into an intentional relationship to the world, a relationship that can, like any other relationship to the world, be performed for performance's sake. For possessing is—in complete contrast to owning—an intentional state in which someone actually has conscious and deliberate control over something. This possessing, like perception, may be performed for the sake of possession, which in turn, in the case of the possession of certain things, leads to an aesthetic experience of luxury. These things are luxury goods—the crucial point being that without the effect of an experience of luxury, these luxury goods would not be luxury goods at all. This is, in any case, the idea that guides this phenomenological description and the reason luxury is considered a form of aesthetic experience. To say it concisely: What for Kant is beauty in the case of perception, is luxury in the case of possession. Neither beauty nor luxury is an effect of sensuality. It therefore needs to be demonstrated: For the experience of luxury, the recipient need not reflect on the matter in the same way as for beauty, but does need to reflect, in a different way, on the sense of an object prior to any luxury judgment. For he has to judge beforehand *whether it is meaningful to go to so much trouble, or whether the effort exceeds what is technically necessary for something, as well as what is anthropologically necessary for someone.* This judgment of something as superfluous, irrational, inappropriate, wasteful and exaggerated, based on reflective powers of judgment, is the condition upon which an aesthetic experience *sui generis* rests in the case of possession. It is in any case given if an object—whether by means of a *consciously disinterested perception* or through an *consciously interested possession*—puts a subject into the special mental state, "a feeling which the subject has of himself,"[11] in Kant's supremely apt formulation. And in fact, just as Kant calls for a description of the beautiful as a "feeling of life" [*Lebensgefühl*],[12] so too does the description of luxury adhere to this distinctly anthropological interest: It concerns an exceptional mental state in which people sense, feel, notice or become aware of that which characterizes human beings as human beings—their freedom. Neither the causality of the world nor the constraints of rationality determine a human being. In moments of experiencing luxury, the living person feels that he or she is alive, and that a person can be reasonable only if he or she is not forced to be reasonable.

**8** Introduction

In this book, luxury is presented as a state of human existence that certainly may be attained by means other than the experience of luxury goods. On the contrary, luxury may be placed in a tradition: Friedrich Schiller finds moments of discovery about being human in play, Ernst Jünger in war and in delirium, and Martin Heidegger in anxiety. But in light of an ever-increasing demand for instrumental rationality and heightened efficiency, luxury in particular seems to gain in appeal as a form of transgression against rationalizing utility. Here the circle closes: For the way this protest against instrumental rationality is to be evaluated, whether one welcomes or rejects it, is another question. This book does not set out to judge luxury, but to try to introduce it. It is about the question "What is luxury?" This should not be understood in terms of a dictionary definition, but in a decidedly radical sense. The method is phenomenological, the topic of the book is anthropological: What does luxury mean for human beings?

## Notes

1 Hume himself changed the title of the essay from "Of Luxury" to "Of Refinement in the Arts" in 1760. David Hume, "Of Refinement in the Arts," in Stephen Copley and Andrew Edgar, eds., *Selected Essays* (New York: Oxford University Press, 1998 [1752]), 167–177.

2 Jean-Jacques Rousseau, *Emile, or on Education*, trans. Allan Bloom (New York: Basic Books, 1979 [1762]), 341.

3 Bernard Mandeville, *The Fable of the Bees, or Private Vices, Publick Benefits*, 3rd edn. (London: J. Tonson, 1724 [1714]), 10.

4 Christine Weder and Maximilian Bergengruen, eds., *Luxus: Die Ambivalenz des Überflüssigen in der Moderne* (Göttingen: Wallstein, 2011).

5 Werner Sombart, *Luxury and Capitalism*, trans. W.R. Dittmar (Ann Arbor: University of Michigan Press, 1967), 5.

6 In particular Christopher J. Berry, *The Idea of Luxury: A Conceptual and Historical Investigation* (Cambridge: Cambridge University Press, 1994).

7 John Sekora, *Luxury: The Concept in Western Thought, Eden to Smollett* (Baltimore and London: Johns Hopkins University Press, 1977); Thorsten Meyer and Reinhold Reith, eds., *Luxus und Konsum: Eine historische Annäherung* (Münster: Waxmann, 2003); Maxine Berg and Elizabeth Eger, eds., *Luxury in the Eighteenth Century: Debates and Delectable Goods* (London: Palgrave, 2003).

8 Theodor W. Adorno, "Veblen's Attack on Culture," 73–94 in *Prisms*, trans. Samuel Weber and Shierry Weber (Cambridge: MIT Press, 1981 [1941]), 83.

9 ibid., 75.

10 ibid., 80.
11 Immanuel Kant, *Critique of Judgment*, trans. by James Creed Meredith, edited by Nicolas Walker (Oxford: Oxford University Press, 2007), §1, 35.
12 ibid., 36.

## PART I

# Play, then war, anxiety and drugs—and now, luxury

# 1

# ANTHROPOLOGY AND THE IDEA OF SELF-EXPERIENCE

## The idea of a substitution

Friedrich Schiller is not especially known for having engaged the philosophical problems or phenomena of luxury in-depth; nor does his literary work contain any description relevant to this topic. And yet it is exactly by returning to Schiller's reflections that someone writing a phenomenology of luxury finds the supporting idea for a proper research perspective. This is the idea that in a philosophical anthropology, luxury would fulfill the systematic function Schiller assigned to play. This programmatic and, possibly, surprising idea could be restated as something like: *Luxury instead of play*. That is to say that the crucial things Schiller says about play, and in particular what he expects of play, apply to the phenomenon of luxury at least as well, if not better. This project of substitution or transformation does in fact rest on an interpretation of Schiller's theory of play. Unlike the usual readings of the theory, however, this interpretation is not primarily concerned with what Schiller understood play to be, or to what extent his distinctly special concept of play may be brought to bear on normal phenomena of play—such as card games or football. Even his concept of playing as a *coincidentia oppositorum* of two basic human capacities—play is, for him, the mental state in which human beings' double, sensual-rational nature is suspended—does not ultimately affect the transformation of Schiller's thoughts under

**14** Play, then war, anxiety and drugs

consideration here. This intended transformation rather raises questions about the reason Schiller came to speak about play at all: What further expectations and hopes did he associate with a theory of play? What systematic role is given to play in his anthropological argument?

This, in any case, is the thesis: In *On the Aesthetic Education of Man in a Series of Letters* of 1795—quite apart from what he says there about particular games—Schiller gives play an epistemic function within an anthropological argument. One can say he instrumentalizes play. Schiller has no interest at all in play for play's sake; he is no ludologist. He comes to speak of play because of his interest in human beings; Schiller is an anthropologist. For Schiller, play is a *phenomenon of presence*; it is an exceptional experience through which it is possible for a human being to perceive and understand his existence as a human being. Among the qualities of the letters in *On the Aesthetic Education of Man* that have still not been appreciated, is that if they are interpreted from a contemporary perspective, they have the potential to answer a far more recent and firmly phenomenological question, one that Schiller would hardly have formulated in this way himself. With Schiller, the vague, impossibly broad goal of understanding *people* becomes a very specific, concrete, question, namely: How can a person describe what it is like to be a human being? Is there an aesthetic experience that can show a human being what makes him human? To say it with somewhat more feeling: Are there moments in life when a human being not only is a human being but also is aware that he is a human being? Can the phenomenal quality of one's own existence be brought to or intensified in consciousness?

## The whole human being

The deservedly most famous sentence in Schiller's *Letters* goes: "man only plays when he is fullest sense of the word a human being, and he is only fully a human being when he plays."[1] Here Schiller is using two equally noteworthy and significant formulations: "in the fullest sense of the word a human being" and "only fully a human being when." If we consider these formulations in light of the classical goal of philosophical anthropology, we see Schiller setting his own course within the field of anthropology. At least in this sentence he is linking anthropology to a question that was new in his time. For the classical

Anthropology and self-experience **15**

goal of anthropology is, and has always been, to answer the question, "What is a human being?" For the most part—although not exclusively of course—philosophical anthropology takes up questions such as: What specific capacities define human beings? or What characteristics set a human being apart from an animal? But when someone like Schiller, in his famous sentence, considers when a human being actually is *completely human*, or when, in a statement, is it explicitly pointed out that a human being is *human in the full sense of the word*, such considerations and statements can hardly be understood as answers to anthropology's classical concerns. They give no definition that indicates what a human being actually is; they are not concerned with the difference between human being and animal. Schiller contends that play allows a human being to be completely human, which means, whatever the exact meaning of the concept of play in this context, in his argumentation it does not fulfill the function of naming the *differentia specifica* that separate human beings from other forms of life. Schiller does not defend the thesis of *homo ludens*, if this concept is understood—as it usually is—to designate the exceptional quality of human beings in comparison to other animals, roughly analogous to the characterization *rational animal*. Were Schiller to assert this thesis, he would have to say that a human being is the only life form to possess the capacity to play. But this is neither Schiller's view, nor is it, *prima facie*, a convincing thesis, since many animals such as dogs and cats at least give the appearance of being able to play.

In short, because play, for Schiller, is not the specific quality that makes a life form human, but is taken instead to be a quality that makes a human being fully human, a skeptical question becomes almost inevitable: Are there half humans? How should we imagine a human being who is not complete, to whom the word *human* applies only partially—that is, someone who does not play? What perfection or completion does a human being in a state of play achieve?

## The whole human being conceived as a balanced human being

A look at research in this area shows that for these questions a certain type of answer predominates. We can easily show it using Schiller's

**16** Play, then war, anxiety and drugs

text, but we would miss an important aspect of his argument. This type of answer can be identified by the use of concepts such as suspension, balance, transmission, reconciliation, relaxation, reciprocity, unification or even mutual completion. However these concepts are being put to use, the following model is always in the background: A human being requires two conflicting abilities, one of which will dominate in that person, almost completely in an unfortunate case. The two facilities are his sensuality and his reason. If sensuality succeeds in gaining power over the whole human being, we will have a beast to contend with, according to Schiller. In a case where reason alone dominates, the person becomes a barbarian, the rather odd term Schiller uses for a rigorously rational human being.

Ordinarily, the dualistic model of a human being determines the concept of the whole being as well. The principle of this concept goes: The whole human being is whole because he is not controlled by just one part. In fact, exactly because he can make two demands for control literally play out against one another, he is free of bias and so a free man. So, to be whole is, for Schiller, to be in harmonious peace with one's divided nature. The key idea in this model is ultimately biological, if not actually medical: The whole human being is one who lives in a species-appropriate way by keeping his conflicting drives in balance.

## The whole human being conceived as a human being with self-experience

In the "14th Letter," at any rate, there is a further description of the whole human being that clearly goes beyond the balance model. There, Schiller links the state of play to more than just a peaceful suspension of antagonistic forces. He turns to the question of what such a person experiences, witnesses and feels when he finds himself in this balanced state of play. One could say that Schiller, with his training as a medical doctor, adds a decidedly phenomenological reflection in order to complete the external medical perspective that therapeutically determines how a person should best live in keeping with the complex structure of opposing drives. Schiller does not explain this in detail, but rather sketches a project that attempts to describe, in first-person singular, what someone living an ideal life from a medical

Anthropology and self-experience **17**

perspective would himself experience and feel in the healthy state of free play. This project can also be formulated in Edmund Husserl's sense: What is it like for someone to live in a balanced way in Schiller's sense? This concerns the subjective quality of experience, the phenomenal, experiential character of being-a-whole-person. At this point the questions on which the text is based changes accordingly: How does a player experience being a player? What phenomenal content does this mental state have for the player himself? What does a person in this state feel and sense? Thomas Nagel would ask: *What is it like to be a player?* Accordingly, the concern is: How does it feel to live in a species-appropriate way?

What is worth noting, however, is that Schiller does not answer these questions as one might expect, namely with such a sentence as: in a state of play, the player is aware of being a player. Nor does Schiller say, even having emphasized it, that in play a human being becomes phenomenally aware of the balance of his double nature. It should be noted, however, that this does not mean he would reject it. Schiller, too, takes the position that a player knows what it is like to be a player. It's just that he does not put any particular emphasis on the statement, first, because it is trivial, and second, because it would deflect him from his real thesis, which says that in a state of play, a human being knows what it is like to be a human being; he gets a kind of intuition in himself about what matters to human existence. That is clearly a far-reaching thesis, bringing aesthetic and anthropological intentions together.

Schiller's argument depends on making two different phenomenal contents equal: Anyone who knows *what it is like to be a player* will, as a result, know *what it is like to be a human being*—although the two are not the same at all. For the concepts, *player* and *human being* have neither the same sense nor the same meaning. So Schiller is, finally, making unlike things the same. For him, the mental state of playing, seen from the subjective perspective of the player, involves becoming aware of more than just the state of play. And this being-more-than is only thinkable because the state of playing, as such, has a symbolic quality for Schiller, through which more can be experienced and observed than just the state of playing itself.

With this, Schiller has given a second answer to the question of what a whole human being is: A whole human being is not whole

**18** Play, then war, anxiety and drugs

only because he has organized his drives in a medically unobjectionable way, but because in bringing his conflicting interests into harmony, he has entered into an exceptional mental state in which he himself feels that he is a human being—that is, in which his specific mode of existence as a living being becomes apparent to him.

## The effect of playing: an experience of self

The difference at hand can be described using the two concepts, *cause* and *effect*: The *cause for* someone finding himself in a particularly healthy state is that the conflicting double nature of human beings has been suspended. This is, in turn, bound up with the effect, which is that this human being experiences his being as human. So the concept of the whole human being refers to not only the unity of two drives, but also to a unity of *being* and perceiving, or more concretely, of *being human* and *perceiving oneself as human*, of *biological being* and *experienced being*. The crucial point is this: Being human in the first sense, namely in the biological one, applies to Schiller as well as to barbarians and savages. But in fact these others are not whole human beings for him because it is not given to them to know what it is like to be human. In Schiller's view, then, they are not human in the full sense of the word.

The extraordinary step in the argument—we might more accurately call it the second part of Schiller's two-part step—can be seen more clearly in comparison with Aristotle. For the first step in Schiller's argument is to be found, in a sense, in the *Nicomachean Ethics*. There, Aristotle is not primarily concerned with the classical question "What is a human being?" Rather he begins, very much as Schiller did, with the question: When is a human being living according to his nature and so species-appropriately? Aristotle's answer is clear: Only a man who is working scientifically and theoretically—at best philosophizing—is using the capacity that distinguishes him from an animal. Aristotle would say, with no ifs, ands or buts: A man philosophizes only when he is a human being in the full sense of the word, and he is only fully human when he is philosophizing. For Schiller, it was barbarians and savages who were not entirely and not properly human; for Aristotle, shockingly, it was slaves and women, making it acceptable, in his view, for them to be

Anthropology and self-experience **19**

treated as they were at the time. Apart from this very ethical position making his ethics highly problematic, we are concerned with the following formal step in the argument. Aristotle, too, develops a concept of the whole human being, and to this extent makes a first step similar to Schiller's; but he did not see it in connection with an anthropological experience of self—at least the writing that has come down to us contains nothing of the kind. In Aristotle, one does not find the idea that philosophy is ultimately a practice of self-experience in which a human being senses that he is a human being. But the search for such a practice, for the *Lebensgefühl* it provides, is typical of Schiller. And as far as the value of philosophy practiced in this way goes, Schiller's view should be clear: He would not say that a human becomes aware or becomes aesthetically more intensely aware of his being human by practicing philosophy. One would have to agree with him on this point: The practice of philosophy does not actually lend itself to such an insight.

One should not quibble about words in the description of phenomenal contents of mental states or, as Schiller would say in a more traditional, but perfectly synonymous way, of states of the soul. Whatever word we choose, for Schiller it is about an awareness of the subjective character, about how something is for someone who is conscious of it: *What it is like to be.* A human being at play is a whole human being for Schiller because this person *feels* himself, *senses* himself, *notices* himself, *experiences* himself, *is aware of* himself, actually experiences for himself that he is a human being.

The reference to self-experience as the essential supplement that enables a human being to be a whole human being is not in conflict with the interpretation based on the model of balance, but does put another, supplementary perspective in play, so to speak. From this perspective, the not-completely-human being is not only an unbalanced human being, but one without self-experience. With this, Schiller turns to the phenomenon of a man who may know how to make a proposition, even be able to bring good reasons and clever arguments to bear on a philosophical discussion, showing how such a being as he is himself is categorically different from other animals. Perhaps everyone has at some point known someone to whom this would apply, a barbarian, in Schiller's sense. But such knowing still does not imply that this man also has a *Lebensgefühl*, that is, his own immediate, phenomenal experience of what it is like to be a whole human being—more precisely, the

**20** Play, then war, anxiety and drugs

experience of being alive at this moment in the world as a human being, freely and autonomously present. Being human has qualities of experience that cannot be found in a propositional definition of human beings. There is, it's fair to say, a certain general antipathy toward theory at the heart of the *Letters*, a real weariness of philosophy. Schiller is no longer looking for theoretically subtle explanations of existence, but for experiences, for a nonpropositional knowledge from one's own experience. For knowledge in the form of a knowing *how it is to be the person one is*, is of a nonconceptual kind. This kind of knowledge by acquaintance is—like all phenomenal knowledge—phenomenologically very exciting, because it is immune to falsification. Perhaps one should not speak of knowledge or insight, but more specifically of familiarity. In any case, it would be meaningless for a person to say of himself that he had witnessed himself or experienced himself incorrectly. A person cannot experience himself incorrectly. But he can have experiences that do not permit him to realize what is specific about being human, namely the freedom human beings have both with respect to laws of causality and to the dictates of reason. This lies in the background of Schiller's question: How does one get this familiarity, this experience of one's own human life? What do you need to do?

In the end it comes down to a simple, somewhat depressing thesis: A person's life is, as a rule, defined by phases of disingenuousness in which that person is in fact human in a biological sense, and presumably healthy, but does not feel and experience himself as a living human being. In such phases he lacks the experience of being human. According to Schiller, this is the case because only in those rare, literally wonderful moments of play does one come to an anthropological self-experience of a particular kind, to one's own, human *Lebensgefühl*, to a perception of existence, to an experience that can—because the concept can be understood simultaneously as *genitivus obiectivus* and as *genetivus subiectivus*—be called a double experience of self, as a *self-made* experience of one's *own self* as a human being. Not as an individual person, it is important to note. For Schiller, only play affords this experience because play is the only species-appropriate state for human beings. Seen in this way, his idea could be stated as: In human beings, the *species-appropriate life* leads to the experience of presence, which is species-appropriate for living human beings. In Schiller's anthropology, play therefore fulfills the unique function of letting people experience and feel their existence as human

Anthropology and self-experience **21**

beings. In play, an individual attains awareness that I, too, am present in the world as a human being. At least a rather short passage in the "14th Letter" may be read in this way.

## Friedrich Schiller's "14th Letter"

Schiller's approach to this work is noticeably hesitant and modest; his readers know, it could be done differently. In fact he refrains here from both apodictic proclamations and from assertions based on a position of informed certainty. Rather he carefully invites reflection on the possibility of there being exceptional moments in human lives, moments in which the man himself becomes—as he then writes explicitly—"sensible of his existence."[2] Schiller is writing in the subjunctive, as if he wanted to say: I myself am not completely certain whether there is or could be such a state of mind. On the one hand, he makes it clear that he is concerned with a relationship not to the world, but to oneself, someone perceives the way he is, his existence, which consists not least in that existence being able to perceive itself. On the other hand, it is also clear that Schiller is luckily not concerned with sense and meaning (*Sinn und Bedeutung*); the theme of the *Letters* is not what later began to be called the meaning of life or of existence. One's own existence is neither explained nor made understandable through the state of play, but rather brought to consciousness, made phenomenally present and palpable. Setting the two concepts *comprehensible meaning* and *aesthetic presence* side by side is a good way of distinguishing between them. It is in any case appropriate and probably no accident that Schiller's *Letters* do not bear the title: *On the Hermeneutic Education of Man*. And that is a good thing, for the experience of one's own playing is said to lend existence not meaning and orientation, but aesthetic presence and perceptual intensity.

In the "14th Letter," Schiller makes use of a subtle escalation that contains the decisive philosophical step. At first he lets his real theme remain rather vague; the broad formulation "sensible of his existence" leaves the exact meaning open. It may be that this person perceives *what it is like to be this individual person*—which would not be saying a great deal—or that he perceives *what it is like to be human; what it is like to belong to this species*—which in fact is a philosophically remarkable premise. And this last corresponds exactly to what Schiller has in

**22** Play, then war, anxiety and drugs

mind: He tests an uncertain idea by running through what it would mean if it were correct. He does not undervalue it philosophically: If such an exceptional mental state really were to exist in human beings, it would have exceptionally broad philosophical consequences. A man "would in such cases, and in such cases only, have a complete intuition of his human nature."[3]

## The challenge of seeing for oneself

The significance of Schiller's thought may also be described in this way: Instead of an anthropology trying to develop the best possible foundation for a propositional definition of a human being, Schiller gives a description of an aesthetic practice from which a person can attain "a complete intuition of his human nature." For Schiller, implementation substitutes for philosophy. The text becomes a kind of travel guide or training manual for the reader, helping him to do what is necessary to have the experiences that Schiller had in a state of play. Schiller might even have characterized his text as being in the tradition of René Descartes, for just as Descartes did in *Meditations*, he challenges the reader to gain a particular experience for himself. The reader is understood to participate in the practice. That is phenomenology in the best sense of the word, at least in the classical understanding of phenomenology as it is presented not exclusively, but with particular clarity, in the early, phenomenological Max Scheler, in his Munich days:

> The meaning of the words a phenomenologist uses and the unities of meaning in his spoken or written sentences do not "say" what he means, so that the listener or reader could in this way get acquainted with an idea that was previously unfamiliar. Rather words and sentences are in this case only challenges and at the same time purposefully chosen incentives for the listener to see for himself what the phenomenologist, in speaking, means — the phenomenologist all the while assuming that the listener could also have seen without words and messages. In other situations, in the sciences and in life, "showing and telling" serve only to support an understanding of the intellectual content immanent in the speech, but here, speech only helps to show something, to make it manifest (tr.).[4]

Anthropology and self-experience **23**

In short: A phenomenological text does not say what a phenomenologist believes to be the case, but rather what the reader must do to experience the "mystery" for himself, which is what is at issue for the phenomenologist. For "these mysteries"—as Merleau-Ponty wrote—"are in each one of us as in him."[5]

This phenomenological aspiration lies at the heart of Schiller's *Letters*: Schiller, too, rhetorically challenges the reader to make the observations in question for himself. He does not try to give detailed descriptions of how someone in the state of play actually feels. His text is a classical *protreptikos*, which is to say: He recommends a practice by means of which anyone could have a particular experience, just as a travel guide typically describes what one could experience in a particular place but does not—as in a novel—analyze this experience in detail. In just this respect there is a basic structural relationship to more than a few artists. Schiller shares with them, and with most phenomenologists, the goal of using their work to make something present to the receiver, that is, to make something perceptible. For the *Letters*, that means, Schiller does not describe what it is like for someone to be in a state of play, but rather describes why someone *should be* in a state of play—namely, so that he himself can feel what it is like to be a human being. In the end, Schiller draws two intentions together as follows: On the one hand, he is not interested in answering the classical question "What is a human being?" in the third person singular; the *Letters* are not an anthropological treatise. But on the other hand, he is not interested in simply describing, in the first person singular, how he himself feels as a human being; Schiller's *Letters* are not testimonials of the kind we know from Jean-Jacques Rousseau. That is the decisive point: Schiller wants to describe where and when any human being can have an experience that offers an aesthetic answer, in the first person singular, to the question "What is a human being?" With this context in mind, one can understand the pathos with which Schiller wrote to Gottfried Koerner in February 1793: "Surely no finer word has yet been spoken by a mortal man that that of Kant, which at once contains the whole of his philosophy: You must determine yourself out of yourself" (tr.).[6] This is the reason Schiller rhetorically promotes play as that mental state in which the one who is playing gets an idea or perception of being that is anthropological in the truest sense of the word. Schiller's term "perception" is not meant literally, not as if human existence could be seen, like a thing in sunlight. His formulation "perception of his humanity" may, in light of the whole

**24** Play, then war, anxiety and drugs

context, be understood proto-phenomenologically, that is, as an anticipation of Husserl's view that categorical intuition is possible, namely as a recognition of something general that is bound up with one's own experience. Yet Schiller—unlike Husserl—stays in the subjunctive. The "14th Letter" reads as if it were describing a premonition that there will one day be a phenomenology of humans, under one condition: "assuming that cases of this sort could actually occur in experience."[7]

## Under anaesthesia

To refine Schiller's thesis of the whole human being, an unconscious person, for example a patient under full anaesthesia, would undoubtedly still be a human being for Schiller, but not a whole human being. In fact it is not an appropriate example of Schiller's incomplete human being because it misses the best part of his thesis. That an unconscious person has no consciousness, and so no phenomenal consciousness of what it is like to be a human being, can be derived in a trivially *analytical* way from the concept of unconsciousness itself. It would be considerably more interesting to reflect on whether it would hold true of someone who was sleeping. But all that aside, Schiller means something else, in fact almost the opposite: He is not referring to the trivial fact that unconscious, anaesthetized people don't play, but pointedly reversing it, insisting that all those who do not play are unconscious, just as though they were anaesthetized—at least in an anthropologically relevant respect: Like anaesthetized people, people who do not play do not sense that they have a human existence, they live in a condition of inauthenticity. Here we see the radical nature of Schiller's approach. For Schiller, all human beings who are not playing are living as if benumbed, as if clouded by drugs and so in urgent need of an aesthetic education, which is more like an aesthetic awakening or sensitizing. Schiller's idea of incomplete human beings is no *a priori* triviality, for he continues to insist that being conscious any which way—that is, finding oneself in one of many possible intentional or unintentional mental states—is not sufficient for a human being to be human in the full sense of the word.

In the winter semester of 1936 to 1937 at the University of Freiburg, Martin Heidegger offered an exercise for beginners on Schiller's *On the Aesthetic Education of Man*. From the students' notes it is clear that by the second session he had come to speak of the central point at issue here.

Anthropology and self-experience **25**

Heidegger, too, begins with the observation that play, for Schiller, is a mental state in which human being can find themselves: "The aesthetic state is, in general, a state of *human beings*." It is followed immediately by the crucial question about how this state is special: "Is it just any old state? One among others?" Through his answer, which Heidegger discussed with the students, he shows himself to be a phenomenological interpreter *par excellence*, one who does not read Schiller primarily according to the model of balance, but who grasps the singular anthropological value of play, its capacity to make human existence aesthetically present: "As we come to see what it is, the aesthetic state will reveal itself to be not just one state among others, but that which constitutes the state of human beings as such" (tr.).[8] In other words: any state of human consciousness may—as Descartes demonstrated—be considered a performative proof of the person's existence: I think, therefore I am. I see, therefore I am. I want something, therefore I am. I doubt, therefore I am. In these mental states—as long as it is about proving my existence, that I am—playing is no exception: *I play, therefore I am.* This is the existentially certain, performative proof of one's own existence through self-experience. But in Schiller's view, it is only in rare and exceptional moments of existence that a person succeeds in personally experiencing, in feeling or sensing what makes someone a human being—exceptional moments that may properly be characterized as pregnant moments.

## The pregnant moment

The concept of the pregnant moment was introduced by Gotthold Ephraim Lessing in his essay *Laocoön: An Essay upon the Limits of Painting and Poetry* of 1766. The expression is still widely discussed—and for good reason. In it one finds an apt term for a simple yet important phenomenon of reception aesthetics. If a story, a process or a procedure is to be depicted in a painting or sculpture, just one moment can be shown. But by no means all the points in this time-based occurrence are equally well suited to depict the whole event. On the contrary, in most stories and events there are just a few moments or phases—although definitely more than one—whose depiction enables the viewer of the picture or sculpture to visualize more than just the one selected moment. In the best case, one hopes that the pregnant moment of an event enables the viewer of the depiction to visualize the whole event. It is, finally, an

**26** Play, then war, anxiety and drugs

intuition of something whole by means of a part. In another terminology, closer to Johann Wolfgang von Goethe, one would address this selected moment as a symbolic moment: The pregnant moment is something *special* that facilitates the depiction of something *general*. But whichever terminology we choose, we are concerned with the same principle in every case: A part or snippet, a still image or a snapshot has the capacity to make the whole phenomenon symbolically present for the viewer.

Lessing's prime example is the ancient Laocoön group. Someone who wanted to depict the struggle of Laocoön and his sons with the snakes could perhaps show it, in its development and in its details, in a film or an essay, explain it, and so make it perceptible to the viewer or reader—with a film, such a struggle could be seen even more exactly than with eyes alone. But someone who wants to make an image, perhaps a painting or sculpture of a struggle or other event, has to choose one moment in the temporal occurrence. For this unavoidable decision, Lessing formulated a rule, or at least a suggestion: The artist—or whoever is making the image—should "choose the most pregnant one, the one most suggestive of what has gone before and what is to follow."[9] There actually is another possibility that Lessing did not consider, namely that an artist might invent a moment that was never part of a real event, because this contrived moment would, in keeping with the principle of the pregnant moment, be in a better position than any real moment to make the whole movement or the whole occurrence present. It is still always the case, as even Georg Wilhelm Friedrich Hegel writes, that, "the whole of the situation or action must be portrayed in its bloom, and that therefore painting must look for the instant in which what preceded and what followed is concentrated in one point".[10]

Although those who describe aesthetic effect of a pregnant moment are fond of returning to formulations such as *the appearance of the whole*, we should not become so enthusiastic as to believe that the perception of the whole could, by means of the pregnant moment, be achieved in the same way it would be in a narrative medium in which a view of the whole occurrence would be given. Here, we need to make a distinction. A viewer of the Laocoön group will not be able to see details of the movement in the struggle with the snakes. With a pregnant moment, it is not about *perception of the whole* in a literal sense, but about *the whole becoming present* through the viewer's imagination—stimulated as well as guided by the image. As in an especially good snapshot of someone,

Anthropology and self-experience **27**

a brief moment is enough to get an idea of the whole person, his character, thinking and behaviour; the snapshot is enough for a gifted novelist to sketch out a life that would be typical for such a person. This is because the pregnant moment has retention and protention for the viewer's imagination. That is, it is an *indefinite* definition, for the pregnant moment certainly does not define definitely what happened earlier and what will come next. But it is still an imaginative affirmation of past and future possibilities. In short, the pregnant moment puts the viewer's imagination on the right track, as Lessing aptly puts it:

> Since the artist can use but a single moment of ever-changing nature, and the painter must further confine his study of this one moment to a single point of view, and their works are made not simply to be looked at, but to be contemplated long and often, it is clear that the most fruitful moment and the most fruitful aspect of that moment must be chosen. Now only that is fruitful which allows free play to the imagination.[11]

To put it another way: In a complex event, the pregnant moment is the moment that allows a viewer, by means of a part of the event, to experience the whole event as if it were occurring in the present. This is also relevant to anthropological thinking.

## The pregnant moment in anthropology

The historical thesis that Schiller deliberately drew from Lessing for his anthropology is of no concern at all here. We are concerned with a structural similarity that can be established from a contemporary perspective and that may serve to determine Schiller's intention. For it is remarkable that Schiller's description of what someone experiences in the special moment of play corresponds, down to the very formulation, to Lessing's expectations for the visual depiction of a pregnant moment. Both Lessing and Schiller describe, respectively, how a "complete perception" (Schiller) of a whole complex structure can be retained, even though what can be depicted is "but a single moment of ever-changing nature" (Lessing). Both are equally persuaded that the issue can only be resolved aesthetically, by choosing a symbolic, that is, a pregnant moment from the structure as a whole.

**28** Play, then war, anxiety and drugs

So a viewer of a painting or sculpture can understand the whole of a depicted event in the same way Schiller hoped a person could understand his own life from a moment of play. The person "would [...] in such cases, and in such cases only, have a complete intuition of his human nature."

With this structural affinity in the background, Schiller's *Letters* seem to be guided by the idea that there are anthropologically pregnant moments in the life of human beings. Play enables the player to perceive his humanity fully, just as the pregnant moment makes it possible to fully perceive whole developments. That means that in the life of a human being there are moments in which an aesthetic realization is reached, a feeling of being human. An anthropologically fruitful moment is, finally, an aesthetic experience that is specifically an experience of presence: A feeling of being human, or of consciously belonging to humanity—or at least a qualitative intensification of this feeling. Such moments are the opposite of a sense experience, for in them being human is not experienced as meaningful, controlled or reasonable. Rather being human is felt on its own—it is irrelevant whether the moment of feeling is reasonable or not. That means, in turn, that these anthropologically pregnant moments would seem to be useful in answering the question, "How can a human being experience for himself what it is like to be human?" Like an artist who seeks to make a whole perceptible through a still image, a human being himself can, in certain moments, become sensually aware of the reality of his own existence. Schiller can definitely be understood to say that artist and phenomenologist ultimately face the same problem. For to be a human being in an absolutely ordinary situation also always means to be different, to find oneself in a flow of constant change and a confusion of diversely identifiable mental states. The parallel is that the possession of consciousness has a way of being given that is readily comparable to the situation of Laocoön during his struggle with the snakes: Everything dissolves, everything changes constantly, many aspects are bound up with one another and unrecognizable in the complex confusion. Lessing's thesis is that the sculptor must therefore look for a pregnant moment with which to exemplify an intuition of the whole event. Schiller's analogous anthropological theory states that anyone who wants to experience for himself what it is like to be a human being must seek out and isolate, within his own stream of consciousness, one exceptional mental state which can produce for him the awareness of his own existence.

Anthropology and self-experience **29**

## The problem of the structural whole

Imagine a banal, but common situation of human existence—for example, *one* cooks, *one* watches television, *one* plans a journey, *one* reads a newspaper, *one* looks for one's key, *one* walks through a town. For the question of what it is like to be a human being, one's own experience of such situations should be evidence for the existence of a principle: A human being is ordinarily not exclusively anything—at least in relation to his state of mind in these situations. Martin Heidegger's descriptions are particularly appropriate here. He himself did not want his descriptions to be understood anthropologically under any circumstances. Nevertheless, in *Being and Time* of 1927 it says, with respect to this phenomenon of human existence: "Being-in-the-world is a structure which is primordially and constantly whole."[12] This means that anyone who is doing something so everyday and ordinary as planning a journey is, while he is doing it, in a state of consciousness Heidegger calls a "structural whole,"[13] and from which single intentional states may only be isolated, conceptually differentiated and individuated *ex post*, never having existed as such independently and separately. But that means—here one can fully endorse Matthias Jung's description of common experience—that "in life, coherence takes precedence over any differentiation of psychic functions or 'aptitudes'" (tr.)[14] which is the crucial formal indication of the human relationship to the world. It applies to existence as it does to being: The whole comes before the parts.

As Heidegger actually also sees, this idea produces serious problems if, say, one poses the simple task of describing what it is like for someone to plan a trip. We can deliberate long and hard about whether human beings can know what it is like to be a bat. But the problems actually begin much earlier. Even in seemingly banal, everyday situations of human existence we are dealing with structural wholes that can scarcely be grasped at all, or only with difficulty. That can be spelled out: In planning a journey, the subject is perceiving, writing, calculating, imagining, looking at images, reading, estimating and judging, searching and finding, collecting and ordering, wishing and hoping—and it is all the while in a state of pleasant anticipation, even if there are some headaches involved. The state of mind is so complex that the only single intentional states that can be differentiated and identified from it—through the making of propositional judgments—are states the subject would not consider differentiated and

**30** Play, then war, anxiety and drugs

identified. Individuation occurs when the person makes propositional judgments about himself, such as: *I look at the catalogue. I read the description of the hotel. I would like to take a trip. I look at the map of the area. I add up the costs. I feel I am in good hands. Looking at a picture of the hotel, I imagine myself on the beach. I look for a better offer. I find the perfect flight. I decide. I am pleased. I have a headache.* As accurate as these self-made descriptions of consciousness may be, they can claim to be true only because these intentional states can be isolated analytically from the complex structural whole that can be described as a structural whole with *I am planning a journey.* But they never exist as such neatly separated states.

With the holism of common experience in the background, a significant proportion of the history of phenomenology seems like a long story about describing isolated intentional achievements that figure in everyday situations. There is a kind of phenomenology of ingredients. These are not descriptions that construct the object to be described from assumptions—in that case it would no longer be phenomenology. Rather they are descriptions of phenomena that exist in this purity only through artificial isolation or abstraction, theoretically, in an analysis. Almost every intentional act involved in the simple planning of a journey as a structural whole—Heidegger would call such a common activity *maintaining existence*—has already found its phenomenological classicist.

Edmund Husserl's *Analysen zur passiven Synthesis* [Analyses Concerning Passive Synthesis] from the 1920s or Maurice Merleau-Ponty's *Phänomenologie der Wahrnehmung* [The Phenomenology of Perception] of 1945 describe the principles that apply to the perception of a desk with a travel catalogue on it. Jean-Paul Sartre's comprehensive study, *The Imaginary*, of 1949 defines crucial characteristics of the illusion and the indications that necessarily accompany a mental state that can be observed in planning a journey, if the traveler has imagined the beach—with or without an image. In his neglected study *Phänomenologie des Wollens* [Phenomenology of the Will] of 1900, Alexander Pfänders gives an outstanding description of the ways and means intentional contents in a state of wanting something are given to the one who wants it, that is, how a holiday is given to someone who wants to take a holiday. If we would like to know what principles affect our own experience of searching for and finding a hotel, Manfred Sommer's study *Suchen und Finden* [Seek and Find] of 2002 remains the classic phenomenological description of yet another way human beings have of being human.

Anthropology and self-experience **31**

The list could easily be extended, but we can already see what these separate studies contribute to the description of consciousness in its everyday way of being: They apply to abstracted states of human existence, but not the being of human existence. Heidegger gets to the point: "To be sure, the constitution of the structural whole and its everyday kind of Being, is phenomenally so *manifold* that it can easily obstruct our looking at the whole as such phenomenologically in a way which is *unified*."[15] The diagnosis is persuasive, as is Heidegger's firm view that there is no solution to this phenomenological problem: To put it negatively, it is beyond question that the totality of the structural whole is not to be reached by building it up out of elements. For this we would need an architect's plan. The being of Dasein, upon which the structural whole as such is ontologically supported, becomes accessible to us when we look all the way through this whole to a single primordially unitary phenomenon which is already in this whole in such a way that it provides the ontological foundation for each structural item in its structural possibility. Thus we cannot interpret this "comprehensively" by a process of gathering up what we have hitherto gained and taking it all together.[16] This means that phenomenological studies that describe what it is like for human beings to be in particular intentional states do not, taken together, describe what it is like to be a human being. Being human is something whole that cannot be assembled from atoms of intentionality, like parts— unless one is describing what it is like to be playing, because this atom can, like a pregnant moment, realize the whole.

## Notes

1 Friedrich Schiller, *On the Aesthetic Education of Man in a Series of Letters*, trans. Elizabeth M. Wilkinson and L.A. Willoughby, eds. (Oxford: Clarendon Press, 2005 [1795]) "15th Letter," 107.
2 ibid., "14th Letter," 95.
3 ibid.
4 Max Scheler, "Lehre von den drei Tatsachen," in *Schriften aus dem Nachlass*, Vol. 1 (Bern: Francks Verlag, 1957 [1911/1912]), 465.
5 Maurice Merleau-Ponty, *In Praise of Philosophy*, trans. John Wild and James Edie (Evanston: Northwestern University Press, 1963 [1953]), 63.
6 Friedrich Schiller, "Brief vom 18.2.1793 an Gottfried Körner," in Karl Goedeke, eds., *Schillers Briefwechsel mit Körner. Von 1784 bis zum Tode Schillers*. Part 2: 1793–1805 (Leipzig: Veit, 1859), 18.
7 Schiller, *Letters*, 95, 97.

**32** Play, then war, anxiety and drugs

8 Martin Heidegger, *Übungen für Anfänger: Schillers Briefe über die ästhetische Erziehung des Menschen* (Marbach am Neckar: Deutsche Schillergeschellschaft, 2005 [1936/1937]), 24.

9 Gotthold Ephraim Lessing, *Laocoön: An Essay upon the Limits of Painting and Poetry*, trans. Ellen Frothingham (Boston: Roberts Brothers, 1887 [1766]), 92.

10 Georg Wilhelm Friedrich Hegel, *Aesthetics: Lectures on Fine Art*, Vol. II, trans. John Knox (Oxford: Clarendon Press, 1975 [1820–1829]), 854–855.

11 Lessing, *Laocoön*, 16.

12 Martin Heidegger, *Being and Time*, trans. John Macquarrie and Edward Robinson (Oxford: Blackwell, 1962 [1927]), §39, 225.

13 ibid.

14 Matthias Jung, *Gewöhliche Erfahrung* (Tübingen: Mohr Sieback, 2014) 37.

15 Heidegger, *Being and Time*, §39, 225.

16 ibid., §39, 226.

# 2

# AESTHETICS AND THE SEARCH FOR MOMENTS OF SELF-EXPERIENCE

## Friedrich Schiller's suggestion: grasp existence in its entirety

Schiller's *Letters* may be read as an answer to the question that was central for Heidegger in *Being and Time*. Since human existence always turns out to be a structural whole, it offers, Heidegger says, an answer to the following question: "Can we succeed in grasping this structural whole of Dasein's everydayness in its totality?"[1] Schiller's inventive answer, new in his time, states: If it is possible at all, then only aesthetically, by each person for himself, by means of the experience of pregnant moments in the structural whole of the commonplace.

In Schiller's view, wholeness cannot be grasped theoretically or ontologically. For him there is no propositionally definable principle of wholeness appearing in all forms of human existence. Approaching from the opposite direction, he isolates an exceptional state in which a human being can have an imaginatively realized intuition of the whole—as in the observation of the depiction of a pregnant moment. Schiller considers any search for the red thread running through the whole to be an exercise in futility. We should instead search for and treasure the moments that realize the whole aesthetically. Schiller's suggestion states: The state of play is—not from an outsider's perspective, but for the player himself—such an anthropologically fruitful pregnant moment.

**34** Play, then war, fear and drugs

If we look in a purely formal way at Schiller's main idea—a human being can have a complete intuition of his humanity in play, and in fact only in play—three theses can be discerned. In fact, Schiller never presented them with as clear distinctions as we might have wished, but they nevertheless need to be discussed separately, particularly at the point when we are looking to Schiller to put luxury in the systematic position held by play.

There is, *first*, Schiller's principal suggestion, that human beings actually do have anthropologically pregnant moments of self-experience, moments in which human beings feel what it is like to be human—moments, that is, in which they feel what they are in their whole lives, even if they do not always feel this way. With this, a claim is made for the existence of mental states that have, in their subjective quality of experience, another meaning for human life as a whole, not to say that they have meaning only because they may be seen symbolically as part of a whole.

This is to be distinguished from Schiller's *second* thesis. It contends that the mental state of play is exactly this pregnant moment in which a human being has a complete intuition of his humanity.

Third, is Schiller's thesis that the awareness of existence is possible "absolutely exclusively" in this one and only condition. He actually claims that a human being is entirely human in only one particular mental state. As he says: *He is entirely human only* [sic!] *when he is playing.*

This differentiation makes it clear that we are dealing with three ideas, to which we might position ourselves in different ways. More specifically, it means that anyone who is not convinced by the first idea—that people have aesthetic experiences of presence and existence in their lives—will not have recourse to Schiller. Yet in accepting this idea, we are not obliged to accept the other two theses. On the contrary, it is worth trying to think whether there is another or even several other conditions that would better fulfill Schiller's requirements. Schiller must be open to questions: Does the state of playing really fulfill the aesthetic and anthropological expectations? Why should a human being experience the state of playing, in particular, as a pregnant moment of his being?

## Why play, actually?

It is well known, and acknowledged by Schiller himself, that the *Letters* owe much to the aesthetics of Immanuel Kant. This applies to the concept

Aesthetics and self-experience **35**

of play in several respects. For Kant, too, play fulfills the function—as he wrote in the *Critique of Judgment* of 1789—of giving human beings a "feeling of life"[2]; according to Kant, a person having an aesthetic experience is in a state of mind in which he can sense the conditions of possibility for cognition and, ultimately, for his own consciousness. One can even go as far as Heidegger did in interpreting Kant, and maintain that it was not Schiller but Kant who was the first one to point out that among many states of mind, there was one "basic state of human being in which man for the first time arrives at the well-grounded fullness of his essence."[3] Kant, too, called this basic state of mind *play*. But both Kant and Schiller are applying the term *play* to something that could hardly be identified with a game. For it is uncontroversial: A tennis player, during a match, would not be in a state of playing for either Kant or Schiller.

Yet, however we evaluate their debt to Kant, the *Letters* offer a thoroughly independent train of thought in support of Schiller's thesis of play as a pregnant moment. It can be summarized as follows: Someone is playing when he is in a state of freedom from one-sided demands, either sensual or rational. For Schiller, only a life-form that is human can be free with respect to the laws of causality and the demands of reason because in his view only human beings are free—a very simple analysis. He draws the following conclusion in support of his thesis about why the mental state of play is an anthropologically relevant pregnant moment: Because a player knows what it is like to be a player, and because this implies analytically that he also knows from his own experience what it is like to be a free being—on the grounds of conceptual presuppositions—a player knows automatically and necessarily from his own observation what it is like to be human.

The train of thought has something persuasive about it, but it is not very helpful phenomenologically because one would simply and urgently like to know when a person is actually playing and what a person must do in order to arrive at the declared intuition of humanity for himself. Would it be better to join a tennis club or an art club? One gets the impression that Schiller took the concept of play over from Kant without reference to actual phenomena or practices, and in the end is using it in a circular way, like a cipher, that is, as a placeholder for the phenomenon that play is thought to make possible. On the one hand, Schiller explains play using the state of being-completely-human: "A human being only plays when he is

**36** Play, then war, fear and drugs

a human being in the full sense of the word" (p. 107). He explains the state of being-completely-human, on the other hand, using the state of playing: *"He is only completely human when he is playing"* (author's italic). In fact, from this sentence, surely Schiller's best known, a reader learns nothing at all about where and when a person finds himself in this exceptional situation, where and when he is completely human or how he can sense his existence, but rather only that he is somehow able to do it and that this state in which he somehow succeeds, should be called *playing*, despite the departure from normal usage. From this standpoint the text seems protreptically bland and empty: Something is being insistently asked of us, and we don't know what it is. In the end, the famous sentence from the "14th Letter" means: *A human being feels his free existence only when he is human in the full sense of the word, and he is only completely human when he feels his free existence.* That means, specifically: The mental state in the life of a human being that meets Schiller's anthropological expectations remains oddly unrecognizable.

## Martin Heidegger: anxiety instead of play

The relation between Heidegger's and Schiller's reflections can be turned around: Just as Schiller's theory of play can be understood as a satisfactory answer to Heidegger's question, "Can we succeed in grasping this structural whole of Dasein's everydayness in its totality?"[1] Heidegger's own answer contains a reflection very much in the tradition of Schiller. One could actually say that both philosophers pursue the goal of describing how "Dasein's Potentiality-for-Being-a-Whole has Existential Authenticity."[4] Like Schiller, Heidegger, too, worked with the image of a whole person, or, respectively, a whole Dasein. But with him, there is a proper substitution for play. The expectations Schiller described with respect to the state of play are, for Heidegger, bound up with another mental state—and this, despite Heidegger's answer, seems at first to give no hint that he, like Schiller, would define a pregnant moment anthropologically.

Heidegger's argument in *Being and Time* begins—in the first of two excerpts—with a distinctly ontological thesis that Schiller would have rejected. As Heidegger himself writes, his aim is "to grasp the totality of this structural whole ontologically"[5]; he is looking for "the formally

Aesthetics and self-experience **37**

existential totality of Dasein's ontological structural whole."[6] To put it more simply: Heidegger is looking not for the pregnant moment, but rather for a kind of red thread that runs through the whole of existence, that is part of every place, that is "essential to every state of mind."[7] The metaphor of a red thread can be used if it is understood in such a way as to mean that redness is present at all the diverse moments of existence. Heidegger would like to identify a phenomenon that onto-logically defines existence in all its forms:

> The being of Dasein, upon which the structural whole as such is ontologically supported, becomes accessible to us when we look all the way *through* this whole to a single primordially unitary phenom-enon which is already in this whole in such a way that it provides the ontological foundation for each structural element in its struc-tural possibility.[8]

The result of Heidegger's search for the "Dasein's primordial totality of being"[9] has become famous. It is called: *Care*. For Heidegger, the being of Dasein is care. Heidegger justifies this with the claim that Dasein must always be understood as something that exists, whose being is about being. "Care, as a primordial structural totality, lies "before" [*vor*] every tactical "attitude" and "situation" of Dasein, and it does so existentially *a priori*; this means that it always lies *in* them."[10] With this it becomes clear that Heidegger is trying to grasp the whole of Dasein by wholly defining what Dasein defines.

It is simply inconceivable that Heidegger would not have noticed that "care" is by no means the phenomenal determinant of all situations in everyday life. In any case, a person is not inclined to care about himself in all situations of everyday life. There are carefree moments. So the previous description of Dasein does not meet Heidegger's own phenomenological demands—at least not yet. A phenomenological description must be grounded in in one's own experience. But it is not a given that Dasein in all its forms will be consistently experienced as Dasein as care. That means, Heidegger, too, must look for a pregnant moment that reveals care aesthetically as the structural whole of Dasein. So, he wants to give an add-itional "phenomenal basis,"[11] a kind of second step following his "answer to the guiding question about the totality of Dasein's structural whole."[11] But this second step is no longer ontological; rather it is decidedly aesthetic,

**38** Play, then war, fear and drugs

even if Heidegger wouldn't have put it that way. One could even say, very much in the tradition of Schiller! For Heidegger, too, is now asking himself whether there are brief, exceptional moments when the existence of Dasein as care is phenomenally revealed. And the answer is, yes, there are such moments, of *anxiety*. For Heidegger "anxiety [is] an exceptional state of mind"[12]; in moment of anxiety, the care structure of the whole of Dasein becomes conscious. In short, what a human being experiences in anxiety for Heidegger, he experiences in play for Schiller.

However, we finally evaluate Heidegger's alternative suggestion— whether we attribute an existentially symbolic dimension to anxiety or not, what matters is the figure of thought. In Heidegger, too, we find the thought that states of mind are not equally effective in revealing Dasein. One could say that compared to Schiller, Heidegger's thesis is: *Anxiety instead of play*. That is to say, a human being is afraid when he is human in the full sense of the word, and *he is only fully human when he is anxious*. In brief moments of anxiety, a human being becomes phenomenally aware of the being of Dasein. For "in anxiety there lies the possibility of a disclosure which is quite distinctive."[13] Anxiety, for Heidegger, is, as play is for Schiller, an exceptional mental state that reveals "the basic possibilities of Dasein," the "possibilities of its being"[14]—and in fact reveals them phenomenally. So, we can say: Anxiety is related to care as a pregnant moment is related to the whole event. Karl Jaspers would speak of existential enlightenment in this way.

In fact we can establish that work with anthropologically pregnant moments determines not only Heidegger's existentialism, but also, in a comparable way, that of Karl Jaspers. For Jaspers, too, exceptional experiences are bound up with the function of transforming mere biological being into human existence, to which an intuition of Dasein as a whole belongs. In the book *Existenzerhellung* [Existential Elucidation], of 1932, Jaspers writes, unequivocally, "To experience border situations is the same as Existenz."[15] But—and this is critical—this insight by way of existential enlightenment does not lead to existential awareness. Existential enlightenment is not self-awareness by means of reflexive self-consciousness, but rather is, for Jaspers too, a kind of aesthetic experience of self. This comes about by means of border situations that for this very reason are, in turn, proper pregnant moments in one's own existence. It is astonishing how clearly the idea of a pregnant moment is again taken up in Karl Jaspers' work. As if he

Aesthetics and self-experience **39**

wanted to allude to this aesthetic phenomenon that Lessing described, he said in a radio lecture in 1951:

> Just as one single peach blossom can realize the whole of spring for a prisoner on break in the prison common, turning a minimum into everything, so do experiences suddenly enter into our being, revealing themselves, unannounced, to those who do not deny them. But this minimum must be palpably there, so that it can be expanded to completeness in fantasy (tr.).[16]

We are concerned with functional equivalents: Heidegger's anxiety, Schiller's play and Jaspers' border situations, namely the death of others, suffering, struggle, guilt—all these exceptional experiences lead to the same extent not to a propositional existential insight, but to an existential illumination. As comparable as these equivalents may be in functional hindsight, however, each has its own counter-connotations in the life world, producing a tremendous difference in the argumentation. In everyday speech, the concept of play—exactly the opposite of anxiety— stands for a positive activity, one bound up with qualities such as joy, amusement, fun and freedom and—very importantly—it is an activity in which one chooses to engage. One decides to play. The exact opposite is the case for anxiety, which is avoided rather than sought; it happens to someone, it occurs involuntarily. Heidegger's suggestion is, therefore, that anxiety is defined not only as a potential way of experiencing an exceptional revelation of existence but, in light of this power to reveal existence, an experience of heightened value, to the point of being represented as a desirable state.

Jaspers' border situations are unavoidable and differ in this respect from extreme situations such as drug highs, fast driving or bungee jumping. For Jaspers, human life necessarily brings border situations; they happen to people—play is different. For Schiller, a person can look for attractive possibilities wherever they may be to reach a state of play. While Heidegger and Jaspers can hardly think of a life without fear and border situations, for Schiller a life without experiences of play is not only thinkable, but, in fact, the rule. One has to do something about it; one must become receptive to it.

**40** Play, then war, fear and drugs

## Ernst Jünger: adventure instead of play

From the title of his book alone, *Kampf als inneres Erlebnis* [Combat as Inner Experience] of 1922, Ernst Jünger's interest in the first person singular perspective is unambiguously clear. This interest persists in *Über den Schmerz* [On Pain] of 1934 and *Annäherungen* [Approaches] of 1970, in which Jünger describes his extensive experience with drugs. Still, whichever of the great themes in Jünger's work may come to mind—whether war and battle, pain and suffering or drugs and intoxication—reading his descriptions with those in Schiller's *Letters* in mind makes it possible to speak of a consistent guiding thought substitution: *adventure instead of play*. It should be noted that Jünger does not use the concept of adventure—a central category in his work—in the playful, touristic way that is now usual, however, but as a synonym for a border experience. For "every adventure," Jünger writes, "lives thanks to the proximity of death, around which the adventurer revolves."[17] His thesis states: "adventure is a concentrated form of life."[18] For Jünger, existential adventure and border situations fulfill the function of an anthropologically pregnant moment. That may be also be the reason so many people find Jünger's books so unpleasant. It seems cynical and inhuman to treat field trenches as adventure. And Jünger does in fact derive something humanly positive from something humanly terrifying—terrifying in a way that is actually completely different from inevitable border situations in Jaspers' sense. What is sought out is rather transgression that people commit more or less deliberately. It is in any case not a *conditio humana* that people must fight wars or take drugs.

Jünger's understanding of the pregnant moment is especially clear, and certainly especially extreme, in the war diary *Storm of Steel* of 1920. Using a bracketing-out technique reminiscent of the phenomenological epoche, Jünger describes having experienced the presence of his own Dasein, which is there beyond and despite all justifiable perceptual doubts and questions. So, even if two books—Schiller's *Letters* and Jünger's *Storm of Steel*—are as different in style, outlook and tone as they could possibly be, they still have a figure of thought in common. Jünger observes and, in fact, goes on to analyze human Dasein, just as Schiller did, from those moments capable of bringing Dasein to self-awareness. Jünger, in *Storm of Steel*, is looking for what Schiller calls, in the *Letters*, an "intuition of humanity." He and Schiller share the view that this intuition is possible only by means

## Aesthetics and self-experience    **41**

of symbolic pregnant moments, and that the goal can be reached only aesthetically. He, like Schiller, also holds the view that although an author may be able to describe these moments, the description does not in itself provide the philosophically appropriate intuition of the human; it gives instructive suggestions about what any one person must do so as to reach a perception of his own existence as being human. Jünger, too, sets out a program—alarming to many people—of aesthetic education in this regard. And, just as for Schiller, these moments are exceptions to everyday experience—although no longer play, as they are for Schiller. Jünger finds the moment of anthropologically significant self-experience first in the trenches and later when high on drugs. According to Jünger, it is at moments of mass murder, hideous brutality and serious threats to one's own life that one can have experiences that are symbolic, because the phenomenal content of such moments is not exhausted by knowing what it is like to be in a trench. It becomes an experience whose enactment Jünger recommends as protreptically and positively as Schiller did for play. Jünger's work has the irritating and shocking effect it often does because the anthropological thesis he implies can readily be reduced, following Schiller, to the statement: A human being fights [*kämpft*] only when he is human in the full sense of the word, and *he is only completely human when he fights.*

On the experience of being under fire, he writes: "Strangely, that moment is one of very few in my life of which I am able to say they were utterly happy".[19] Jünger's justification for this feeling of happiness follows immediately in the next sentence. It is no glorification of war for war's sake, however, but rather an identification of war as a means of getting the anthropological experience. He writes: "I understood, as in a flash of lightning, the true inner purpose and form of my life."[19] Since Jünger, like quite a few authors of his time, uses the concept of *Gestalt* as a synonym for *essence* or *idea*, we can say that at such a moment Jünger is getting what Schiller calls an intuition of humanity. Jünger's conclusion therefore states: to one who would grasp "life in its innermost form," war—like other experiences of existential limits— offers a possibility. The adventure of a boundary experience—ecstasy, state of intoxication, pain—for him are mental states "which show the meaning of a human being" (tr.), which is the first sentence of *Über den Schmerz* [On Pain].[20] It is a formulation that really might have been used by Schiller as well. But it is not the formulation that is crucial. It is rather the substitution made here for play with a new functional

**42** Play, then war, fear and drugs

equivalent, which, with Schiller's help, might be stated as follows: A human being has a boundary experience only when he is human in the full sense of the word, and *he is only fully human when he is having a boundary experience.* Jünger insists that this must be accepted, for only one's own experience fulfills the radical epistemological demand for absolute certainty. In *Annäherungen* [Approaches] of 1970, Jünger makes this protreptic aspect explicit, as an invitation to take drugs as a boundary experience. As Descartes asks his reader to carry out each meditation for himself so as to experience for himself that his existence cannot be doubted, so Jünger demands, in the Cartesian tradition, that each reader must have his own adventure and survive it in order to have his own experience of what it is like to be human:

> My real task was not intended to be so much to write a book as to construct an artifact, a vehicle from which one departs as a different person from the one who boarded it. This also applies to the author: *meditations ad usum proprium*, for his own orientation. A reader may participate according to his tastes or his needs.[21]

## The many pregnant moments

Heidegger's and Jünger's reflections provide exemplary evidence that various mental states can serve the anthropological function of Schiller's play equally well—and that all pregnant moments are by no means of equal value at all times. This insight opens the history of anthropological thinking to the question of who, when and why other mental states have been suggested as anthropologically relevant pregnant moments. A few suggestions come to mind that are surely worth examining more closely, for example, the question of whether this function was first attributed to the sublime by Kant or by postmodern readers at a later time. It would be worth analyzing the extent to which an anthropologically pregnant moment is described in works within Marxism: *Does a human being work only when he is human in the full sense of the word, and is he only fully human when he is working?* In the lecture *Die Grundbegriffe der Metaphysik* [The Fundamental Concepts of Metaphysics] of 1929–1930, Heidegger too seems to raise a question about whether anxiety has to be understood as the one and

Aesthetics and self-experience **43**

only anthropologically decisive pregnant moment, as previously maintained in *Being and Time*. He makes this view relative, at least what he had said earlier about anxiety he says here about profound boredom: "This boredom reveals what-is in totality."[22] It is the second possibility for an "awakening" from everyday inauthenticity[23] so to speak, for "this attunement brings us ourselves into the possibility of an *exceptional understanding*."[24] It "has in itself this character of manifesting how things stand concerning us."[25] All of these are functional equivalents. Hans Ulrich Gumbrecht recently made an innovative suggestion very much in this tradition: That there are "moments of being lost in focused intensity while watching sports,"[26] that offer an anthropological experience of presence—it is worth noting that this applies to both athlete and observer.

But apart from whether and where and how often the search for substitutes strikes pay dirt, once it is thinkable in principle for the function of play in Schiller to be taken over by other mental states, the question arises of how one is to deal with this plurality of functional equivalents. Does the *tertium non datur* apply? That would mean: If Schiller is right, then he is simply the only one who can be; then various pregnant moments would mutually exclude one another. This brings us to a problem familiar from art history.

## An example from art history: the double pregnant moment

A sculptor is constrained by the topic: If the story of David from the Old Testament is to be depicted, a moment from the event needs to be specified. At least three suggestions have become classics in this regard: In the early Renaissance, around the mid-15th century, Donatello presents a childlike David *after the great battle*, wearing only a hat and contemplating his foot on Goliath's severed head, bowed, weak in the knees, but incredibly cool. Fifty years later, in the High Renaissance, Michelangelo presents David as a vigorous young man— without a hat, but with locks to make up for it—in a phase of mental anticipation of the event, at the moment of the greatest concentration before the actual battle: Gazing into the distance, suspecting what is to come, seeing and planning. Once again, a good hundred years later, around 1625 in the Baroque, Bernini chooses that moment for

**44** Play, then war, fear and drugs

his sculpture in which an extremely excited, athletic and energetic David, an adult man at last, is pulling a sling back to its most extreme point *during the battle*, so as to whip the sling forward in the opposite direction with his arm and his whole body in the next moment.

Assuming we take the view that these sculptures, although they depict different moments, are equally well suited to present the battle as a whole—in the sense of an imaginative realization, the question arises: How are these three pregnant moments related to one another? We can think of at least two basic positions.

First: The three moments are three possibilities given in principle; for an event possesses several points that serve the function of realization equally well. In this case we interpret the multiplicity as the possibilities for the depiction of a story that these artists discovered, produced and confirmed; there are three moments that are equally effective in concentrating the event.

Second: There are several pregnant moments; but they differ historically and culturally; they do not have the same meaning at every time and in every culture. Which moment is most effective when and where therefore does not depend solely on the event to be depicted. In his sculpture, Bernini does discover one of several possible ways of condensing the events that were available, in principle, at any time. For historical and cultural reasons these possibilities were not available to Donatello; they were typical, on the other hand, in Bernini's time. In this reading, any pregnant moment is a *doubly* pregnant moment: Bernini's moment of exaggerated movement is a symbol that condenses and presents, first, the David story and then the zeitgeist of the Baroque. To put it another way: Both Michelangelo's *David* and Bernini's *David* bring the story imaginatively to life equally well for a viewer. But the sculptures are so powerful in their differing choice of pregnant moment that the *David* of Michelangelo best lets us experience the whole culture of the Renaissance, and that of Bernini, best the whole Baroque. The different pregnant moments from the same story are themselves, in turn, pregnant moments in different ways of thinking, times and cultures. Not every possible solution available in principle at any time is an appropriate solution for every zeitgeist. A comparison between Michelangelo and Bernini makes this especially easy to see.

Aesthetics and self-experience  **45**

Someone who wants to know what the Renaissance is can reconstruct it, with a little imagination, from Michelangelo's *David*: The Renaissance is a way of thinking that is not restricted to art. It is the expression of a culture of planning and mathematical rationality. It prioritizes the idea of reality: Renaissance is the rationality that defines actions—such as the production of art—in terms of concepts, and that takes the concrete realization of an action to be something that follows, a version secondary to the real thing. The intellectual idea, the reasoned plan, the elaborated concept, is more highly valued than the transformation into practice. One can even say that in the Renaissance, the actual work is *disegno*, the plan, the drawing, a reduction to essentials. It takes the same view Lessing represented in the tragic drama "Emilia Galotti" of 1772 by formulating—as a kind of aesthetic thought experiment—a question whose answer goes to the heart of Renaissance thought. "Do you not think," he asks, "that Raphael would have been the greatest genius in painting, even if he had had the misfortune to be born without hands?"[27] From a Renaissance standpoint, the answer is unequivocal: Yes! The craft of transformation can be left to others, to Raphael's workshop, for example. The key point is that the same attitude governed Michelangelo's choice of pregnant moment for *David*'s ideal form: Through the choice of this particular moment, the sculpture brings this attitude to view, like a second pregnant moment in a sense. In this way the pregnant moment itself becomes another pregnant moment: In the choice of this moment, the sculpture exemplifies the typical thinking of the Renaissance, which considers the decisive part of an action to be the plan, the concept, the idea, the will. In this sense, this pregnant moment in the David story was chosen and depicted as the pregnant moment of the artist's own time. The viewers can imagine how the struggle between David and Goliath played out; no artist is needed for that. An ordinary imagination is enough. So this sculpture shows something that holds for Renaissance rationality as such—that the rational idea is valued more highly than its ephemeral execution; that what someone intends, his reasoned-out plan, is the deciding factor in an action. Yet this is exactly what the Baroque sees differently, as Bernini's *David* shows very well.

The less than ideal reality of the individual action becomes the decisive moment of the action. The Baroque is a culture of the ephemeral, the

**46** Play, then war, fear and drugs

momentary: Abundance rather than reduction; accident rather than planning, contingency instead of logic, conflict rather than perfection. One does not conform to plans and prescriptions. What is relevant is not what one wants, but what one does. Once we know what someone is doing, it is easy to imagine the motivation, the plan he had—and if he had none, it's no longer an issue. The main thing is that the right thing is not thought but done. It is not the timeless idea, not the *disegno* that determines the value of a work, but its ephemeral coloration. No drawing has ever become a painting without color. So color becomes the essential thing in an image, a position borne out in rebellion against the dictatorial power of mathematics, planning and the canon. This rebellion defines the thinking of the Baroque and can, with a little imagination, be seen in its great works of art as in a pregnant moment. These are the Baroque masterpieces, as Friedrich von Schlegel aptly put in in the "Athenäums Fragmenten" [Fragments from the *Athenaeum* journal] of 1798, "through the surprising randomness of their production, through the deductive treatment of ideas, and through the Baroque of the dashed-off expression" (tr.).[28] That which is changeable, ephemeral, transitory becomes the essential thing—as in the moment chosen in Bernini's sculpture. From the David story, it is the concrete action that is chosen, the point in the athletic movement that even without movement exists only as an asymptotic transition between two opposed movements, in which the halted motion backward becomes the beginning of a forward motion; an ephemeral, contradictory moment that doesn't actually exist: A short, a Baroque moment of peace in the greatest turmoil, a racing stillness.

## The search for the pregnant moment

If we apply the idea of the doubly pregnant moment to Schiller and Heidegger, that is, to the pregnant moments they favored, *play* and *anxiety*, things go wrong. These exceptional mental states are meant to be aesthetically effective moments, but the aesthetic effect of these moments is, for Schiller as well as for Heidegger, temporally and culturally invariable. Play, for Schiller, is play with transcendental features everyone has, and so not historical. Schiller does not want to say that, at this time, some people are socialized in such a way that they can perceive their existence as a human being in play. But that is an idea that must be taken seriously. Can't that which functions as an anthropologically

## Aesthetics and self-experience   **47**

pregnant moment change, be suggested or in fact provoked by a society? Doesn't the search for an anthropologically pregnant moment have to lead to different results at different times? Could there not be a cultural history of anthropologically pregnant moments, analogous to examples from the history of art? There are, finally, historical and cultural constellations that make other experiences anthropologically productive, perhaps not for everyone, but for many. That is: The determination of the pregnant moment is an aesthetic decision that depends on the time, fashions and discourses, social conditions and concepts of style, on idiosyncrasies, expectations, cultural values and individual preferences. That is: Whatever actually serves a society in the capacity of a pregnant moment of self-awareness is itself the aesthetic expression of a cultural present as well. The phenomenological description and definition of a pregnant moment therefore is—as in art—an effort to catch the spirit of a time.

Someone who sets out to find a pregnant moment is taking on an aesthetic task that always requires a fresh approach. This is an idea that is perhaps most readily observed in Ernst Jünger's work. His movement from themes of war, pain and battle to the descriptions of highs and drug consumption may also be taken as confirmation that the anthropologically pregnant moment should always be understood in a double sense as a pregnant moment of its time and the changing life-forms in it. As a site of aesthetic experience of self in a liberal society, the appeal of the field trench has, happily, diminished sharply. It is hardly sought out for the sake of aesthetic experience at all. Even if it does still possess the power of a pregnant moment to reveal existence—as Jünger described it—it seems obsolete today.

Another contest for a David sculpture should be held. With no final, culturally fixed and absolute solution of the way a person can experience himself in pregnant moments in mind, without even the belief in this perspective, the lived aesthetic practices of the time become important. Even Schiller understood his own suggestion of becoming aware of one's humanity through play to be a diagnosis of his time: Namely as an explicit reaction to the French Revolution. Exactly because life-forms and life-worlds change—luckily not only through revolution—there is also a change in the places where large and small groups look for the presence of being, of existence, the intensification of one's own awareness of being human.

**48** Play, then war, fear and drugs

With this in the background, it is worth trying to relate anthropological thought in the tradition of Schiller to current social conditions. Where can one have the experiences Schiller saw realized in play? Specifically: If we perceive the life world to be governed by utilitarian thinking, what constitutes, or at least starts to be attractive as, an anthropologically pregnant moment? The changes under consideration here are not new and have descriptions that are as accurate as they are critical.[29] The question arises: Where do anthropologically pregnant moments go when a life world is controlled by a ubiquitous logic of escalation, a pervasive demand for optimization, a proliferating utilitarianism, a comprehensive regimentation of time? How do people react in their search for an existential experience of being when practicality has become the highest cultural priority? It would be extremely surprising if economizing in a society did not elicit aesthetic practices as reactions, determining how and where people under these social conditions can experience, in pregnant moments, what they continue to be in spite of all instrumental reason: Human beings, determined by neither the laws of nature nor commandments of reason. With this in mind, what follows will be—as it was for Schiller—about the presentation and defense of two theses that blend together in the course of their description: That is, about the designation of *two* pregnant moments. In the foreground is the description of an anthropologically pregnant moment that is possible in principle. But all the while it is obvious that such a phenomenological description, today, is itself an aesthetically presented diagnosis of the time, one that produces—exactly by identifying it—an awareness of the immanent structure of a social condition. In short, this thesis states: Since Schiller, Heidegger and Jünger, different life experiences hold out hopes for an intensification of existence. First play, then war, anxiety, drugs—and now, luxury. The priority of instrumental reason can be observed in its effects on many social contexts; it shows not only in planned effects, however, but also in unplanned side effects, for example in the attraction of luxury as a liberating, emancipatory transgression against utilitarian reason: A human being experiences luxury only when he is human in the fullest sense of the word human, and *he is entirely human only when he is experiencing luxury*.

## Notes

1 Heidegger, *Being and Time*, trans. John Macquarrie and Edward Robinson (Oxford: Blackwell, 1962 [1927]) 39, 226.

Aesthetics and self-experience **49**

2  Immanuel Kant, *Critique of Judgement*, trans. James Creed Meredith, revised by Nicolas Walker (Oxford: Oxford University Press, 2007) §1, 35, 36.
3  Martin Heidegger, *Nietzsche, Vol. 1: The Will to Power as Art*, trans. David Farrell Krell (San Francisco: HarperCollins, 1991 [1936–1939]), 113.
4  Heidegger, *Being and Time*, §62, 352.
5  ibid., §41, 235.
6  ibid., §40, 237.
7  ibid., §40, 235.
8  ibid. §39, 226.
9  ibid., §39, 227.
10  ibid., §41, 238.
11  ibid., §40, 229.
12  ibid., §40, 233.
13  ibid., §40, 235.
14  ibid.
15  Karl Jaspers, *Philosophy, Vol. 2: Existential Elucidation*, trans. E.B. Ashton (Chicago and London: The University of Chicago Press, 1970 [1932]), 179.
16  Karl Jaspers, "Mein Weg zur Philosophie," in *Rechenschaft und Ausblick: Reden und Aufsätze* (Munich: Piper, 1951), 329.
17  Ernst Jünger, *Approaches: Drugs and Ecstatic Intoxication*, https://archive.org/details/ApproachesDrugsAndEcstaticIntoxicationErnstJunger1/page/n7, n4, accessed 19 December 2018 [1970].
18  ibid., n5.
19  Hoffmann (London: Penguin, 2004 [1920]), 281.
20  Ernst Jünger, "Über den Schmerz," in *Sämtliche Werke*, vol. 7 (Stuttgart: Klett-Cotta, 1980 [1934]), 145.
21  Jünger, *Approaches*, n8.
22  Martin Heidegger, "What is Metaphysics?" in Stefan Schimanski, eds., *Existence and Being*, with introduction by Werner Brock and trans. R. F. C. Hull and Allan Crick (Chicago: Henry Regnery, 1949 [1929]), 364.
23  Martin Heidegger, *The Fundamental Concepts of Metaphysics: World, Finitude, Solitude*, trans. William NcNeill and Nicholas Walker (Bloomington and Indianapolis: Indiana University Press, 1996 [1920/1930]), 59.
24  ibid., 136.
25  ibid.
26  Hans Ulrich Gumbrecht, *In Praise of Athletic Beauty* (Cambridge and London: Harvard University Press, 2006), 55.
27  Gotthold Ephraim Lessing, "Emilia Galotti" in *Five German Tragediess* (Harmondsworth: Penguin, 1969 [1772]), 37.
28  Friedrich von Schlegel, "Athenäums Fragmente" in Ernst Behler and Hans Eichner, eds., *Kritische Schriften und Fragmente: Studienausgabe*, vol. 2 (Paderborn: Ferdinand Schöningh, 1988 [1798]), 125.
29  Hartmut Rosa, *Weltbeziehungen im Zeitalter der Beschleunigung, Umrisse einer neuen Gesellschaftskritik* (Berlin: Suhrkamp, 2012).

# PART II

# Luxury

The Dadaism of possession

# 3

# THE JUDGMENT OF LUXURY

## The matters at issue and the sense of the concept

In turning to the question "What is luxury?" we can distinguish between two basic possible readings. The first takes the question to be concerned with the things the concept of luxury refers to; we could speak of the *extensional* understanding. Someone who understands the question this way will name objects and lifestyles, furnishings and expenditures that could or should be designated as luxury. Villas, records, confections and *haute couture* could be considered luxuries. The question "What is luxury?" would then be answered in an art, design, or cultural historical sense, by writing a history of special luxury goods. This way of approaching the topic has an academic tradition. Think of Henri Baudrillart's four-volume *Histoire du luxe privé et public, depuis l'antiquité jusqu'à nos jours* of 1878. This tradition has by no means disappeared—on the contrary, it persists, not least in countless coffee-table books that approach luxury by describing luxurious objects, ordinarily using many illustrations and little text.

There is also a second reading of the question that is concerned with what someone knows when he knows that something is a luxury. That is, what is being said about these objects under the circumstances? What is being said to a person when he hears that opera houses are a luxury? We would like to know what the case is if we are to justifiably call something a luxury. This way of reading the

**54** The Dadaism of possession

question—the *intensional* way—complements the extensional understanding, and it would be absurd to think that both perspectives could be aligned with respect to the same phenomenon. The themes are different: One is concerned with history and the qualities of luxury goods; the other is concerned with the sense of the concept of luxury, with its content—that is, with what is, or should, ordinarily be found in a lexicon as the definition of the concept.

Someone who reads the question about luxury intensionally, as a question of content, is not interested in luxury objects themselves, but in the relationship of the concept of *luxury* to other concepts. Actual luxury objects themselves serve, at most, as examples to use in examining the strengths and weaknesses of an understanding of the concept. The goal of the reflection is to develop a clear category that offers possibilities for nuanced and exact description: Whether the purposes are aesthetic, cultural or anthropological—or even simply that someone would like to know what in human life can rightly be designated as luxury. What applies to the concept of luxury holds for the use of any such concept: A statement and description gains precision if conceptual distinctions are made. For example, is a noisy party with culinary delicacies to be considered sheer *extravagance* or should one conclude that it is *mannered, pretentious, pompous, beautiful, pleasant, stylish* or *decadent*, that is has a particular style—or, in fact, that this party is pure *luxury*? Someone who understands the question about luxury in the intensional sense would like to make significant distinctions among these categories; in doing so, he has an expectation that it is worth the trouble to define the sense or content of the concept of luxury more exactly, because this makes descriptions possible that cannot be achieved with any other concept. This refers to the hope that with the concept of luxury—and with it alone—we can identify and address a phenomenon that certainly overlaps with and bears similarities to other phenomena, namely the *beautiful*, the *exalted*, the *elegant*, the *pretentious*, the *comfortable*, the *useless*, the *decadent*, the *grandiose*, the *kitschy*, the *opulent* or the *superfluous*—but that despite all comparability still turns out to be a phenomenon *sui generis*. In other words, a classical thesis of irreducibility will be defended here: No substitutions can be made for the concept of luxury, nor can it be traced back to any other concept.

The judgment of luxury **55**

Sometimes it is possible to detect an explicit resistance to making conceptual distinctions, especially in cultural studies' contexts. It is sometimes said that clear conceptual differentiation implies a belief that the world, too, consists of clearly differentiated phenomena. The assumption makes no sense, however, in fact the opposite is the case: Clear intensional differentiation is needed exactly when the goal is to describe the unclear, ambivalent and layered aspects of aesthetic phenomena. There are things that are beautiful as well as luxurious, which does not make the two qualities the same, and which above all does not mean that the concepts *beauty* and *luxury* are indistinguishable. Other things are both kitschy and luxurious, which does not make the two qualities the same either, although the one thing may have both qualities simultaneously. Other things, in turn, are both ostentatious and beautiful, but cannot be designated luxuries. Approaching with clear conceptual distinctions has the benefit of facilitating descriptions of ambivalent and hybrid mixed forms, the fascinating, manifold phenomena in their various aspects. We are not simply throwing things together, and this is as it should be: The discussion of the phenomenon of luxury suffers particularly from inadequate differentiation. It is easy to see this from the way the concept is used as a synonym for comfort in one place and for pretentiousness in another, depending on what basic convictions the user holds about the world.

In a certain sense, working on a concept of luxury recalls Immanuel Kant's view in his *Critique of Judgment* (1789). For there, Kant points out that the concept of beauty makes it possible to describe a pleasure in things that is categorically rigorously distinguishable from sensual pleasure in things that are pleasant—although he also knows that this linguistic difference is scarcely respected in everyday speech. There, things are very often designated as beautiful when they should, he says, be called *pleasant*. But Kant is not concerned in this text with describing how the concept of the beautiful is *actually* used. He is rather concerned with the way it should be used, so that the sense of the concept, its intrinsic possibilities for differentiation, are not wasted. This exact situation applies to reflection about the concept of luxury as well, which is the reason it, like the concept of beauty, is a genuine philosophical theme. Philosophy is, in any case, the classical discipline for questions about the sense of categories, that is, for work on a concept that facilitates the clearest possible description of the unique features of things and actions, but also of aesthetic experiences, mental conditions and subjective responses.

**56** The Dadaism of possession

Despite this expectation, philosophy has shown almost no interest whatsoever in the concept of luxury. This must concern the concept itself—or more precisely, the marked prejudice found in philosophy with respect to this concept. It states that the content of this concept is easily defined; it is semantically uncomplicated and raises no problems. Problems may arise from moral questions, whether luxury should be welcomed or condemned. There is a plenitude of literature along these lines. There have also been exhaustive disputes about the economic relevance of luxury. Yet—the unspoken prejudice goes—it does not take a philosopher, only a look in the dictionary, as noted, to define the sense of the concept of luxury. The view is widespread in philosophy that concepts readily definable in dictionaries do not constitute serious themes. In his lecture, "Philosophische Terminologie" [Philosophical Terminology] of 1968, Theodor W. Adorno defended this view. He argued in detail that philosophers try, in a kind of pitiable Sisyphean labor, to work out definitions for concepts that cannot be defined. And so there is no progress in philosophy. Rather, there is always another effort to solve, from the beginning, a problem that is unsolvable in principle.

Whatever one may think of Adorno's novel view of philosophical activity, it does help to understand the disinterest philosophers have in luxury. For, if philosophers really try, again and again from the beginning, to define the sense of such intractable categories as *the beautiful, the true* and *the good*, the concept of luxury cannot be a philosophical theme. Philosophers examining philosophically relevant categories do not arrive at definitions suitable for a lexicon, but rather offer complex reflections, at best conducive to understanding the concept, but persuasive only in conjunction with the philosophical theory as a whole. But that is exactly what ought to be fundamentally different for the concept of luxury—as the prevailing view has it—because here a good lexicon is enough. So the sobering conclusion that must be drawn from the history of philosophy is: The question "What is luxury?" is not considered a serious topic. At least this assessment applies as long as we ignore one small, but noteworthy, exception. The reference is to Albert Görland, a philosopher active in Hamburg, who published the programmatic essay "Über den Begriff des Luxus" [On the Concept of Luxury] in 1926 in the journal *Kant-Studien* [Kant Studies]. Like his entire philosophical work, this essay has had no discernible reception or effect, which is regrettable, at least in the case of this essay. For in it, Görland remarks, vividly recalling Adorno's view of the philosophically

The judgment of luxury **57**

relevant concepts, "The concept of luxury is one with an inexhaustible attraction, so that the end of any argument has the character of an abandonment rather than of a conclusion" (tr.).[1] In fact, hardly any other outline of a philosophical research project on luxury can be found. We are dealing here with a completely isolated call from a neglected philosopher, who wants, just for once, to finally describe luxury rather than condemning it morally or praising it economically. Görland explicitly claims "to explain, on a purely phenomenological basis, what is meant by 'luxury.'"[2] Still—and it must be said—his call had no resonance whatsoever— neither among phenomenologists nor among other philosophers; Görland himself made no further effort to pursue his project for a philosophy of luxury. His brief interjection changed nothing about the prevailing view: The concept of luxury is not perceived to be a philosophical or categorical problem. If someone takes an interest in luxury, the question about what luxury is becomes a definition problem that is easily solved. Usually, a sentence is enough.

## The standard definition

One suggestion for a definition of luxury has become famous: It comes from Werner Sombart. The sociologist opens his section "Begriff und Wesen des Luxus" [The Concept and Character of Luxury] from his noted work *Luxus und Kapitalismus* [Luxury and Capitalism] of 1913, with a perfectly normal definition: "Luxury is any expenditure that exceeds necessity."[3] This pinpoints the standard understanding of the concept—and one has to agree with Sombart: This is the sense in which the concept is ordinarily used in everyday speech as well as in scholarly texts. Luxury goods are, accordingly, the objects and lifestyles that exceed the usual notions of what is necessary, what is meaningful, what is normal and appropriate—depending on the situation. Contexts, cultures and situations may change; what was once a luxury need not always be one. But the following applies in any case: If something is a luxury in a particular situation, it is because this something is bound up with an exaggerated, extravagant and superfluous effort. In luxury, notions of what a person actually needs and must have to live are deliberately transgressed. Luxury is consciously extravagant, unrestrained and irrational, and, as such, very definitely always the opposite of simple, economical, objective, efficient and modest.

**58** The Dadaism of possession

Yet as entrenched as Sombart's understanding of luxury may be, this standard definition is only persuasive to a point—namely only so long as we understand the suggested definition exclusively as the definition of a *necessary quality* of luxury; however, this lies beyond the sense of what Sombart was saying. From his standpoint, the definition is sufficient. Only it is easy to show through examples that this is not the case. For it would make no sense at all to speak of luxury whenever anything at all exceeds the necessary. In fact another criterion is needed—the *differentia specifica*—that is adequate to achieve a further focus on particular cases of an unnecessary and irrational effort. Only it does make sense to describe some superfluous effort as luxury. This becomes clear if we think about those forms of sheer waste through straightforward inefficiency that people rightly do not normally call luxury.

If someone is using an antiquated heating system in an apartment building, and for this reason uses appreciably more oil than is technically necessary, pays appreciably more money than is necessary and, on top of it all, invests far more time and effort in constant repairs to the dilapidated heating system, one would still not speak of possessing such heating as a luxury. Others might actually heat a villa with a pool with the same quantity of oil. But this is just a reason to designate the system as wasteful of oil, time and money, hardly for designating it a luxury—although it pointlessly wastes money and oil and only works with great effort. It concerns the sense of the concept: If we designated such an obsolete heating system a luxury, the unsatisfactory result would be to lose the sense of a distinction between the concept of luxury and the concept of inefficiency or wastefulness. In short, it is worth noting something to be found under the entry for *luxury* in—believe it or not—the 242-volume *Oeconomischen Encyklopädie* [Encyclopedia of Economics] of 1801 by Johann Georg Krünitz: "Any luxury is a waste, but not every kind of waste is therefore also a luxury" (tr.).[4]

## Luxury *versus* comfort

Here is the result: From the standard definition à la Sombart, we still have the task of defining the specific kind of waste that distinguishes luxury from other kinds of waste. Yet whatever may emerge from

The judgment of luxury    **59**

this effort to make the question more precise, we can already clearly define *what luxury at this point no longer can be*—on the sole grounds of the characteristics it must have—and considering the way the concept is used in everyday speech, we need to set this boundary as quickly as possible in the interests of avoiding misunderstandings from the start. This concerns the difference between *luxury* and *comfort* on the one hand and between *luxury* and *ostentation* on the other. Although it is not unusual for either concept to be used as a near synonym for luxury in everyday speech, this cannot be reconciled to the idea that luxury must be characterized by a particular kind of excessive effort and, so, of irrational extravagance. This is not to deny that the phenomena of luxury, comfort and ostentation often appear together and mingled. In fact, we are concerned with three phenomena that at least on occasion can be observed in one and the same thing. But that is often the case: One and the same piece of music can be boring and sad at the same time without anyone claiming that sad and boring are the same thing. In this sense, the concepts luxury, comfort and pretentiousness do not signify the same things, even though they are often used to describe the same objects. This can be made more specific as follows: Even if all luxury goods of the world were comfortable or all luxury objects were ostentatious, each concept would be claiming something different about these things.

The relationship between the concepts of luxury and comfort is the theme of Horst Mühlmann's eponymous doctoral dissertation in linguistics of 1975. Although the impressive wealth of examples the author presents is now dated, as one would expect, the work's main thesis remains in general completely persuasive. This thesis is that we are dealing with a linguistically rare and exceptional situation, in fact with a paradoxical one: Although the concepts luxury and comfort are proper antonyms in terms of their content, they are nevertheless used in everyday speech—not exclusively but additionally—as synonyms, even though the lexical difference is actually quite easy to define:

> If "luxury" figures into the construction of the semantic field *abundance/extravagance*, "luxury" and "comfort" are in semantic opposition: with "luxury," components such as *uselessness, redundancy, inefficiency* are the most prominent; with "comfort," it is

**60 The Dadaism of possession**

> components such as *usefulness, necessity, efficiency*. [...] On these grounds, the words "comfort" and "luxury" are antonyms (tr.).[5]

This is contradicted, however, by Mühlmann's well-supported observation that a person who says *that is a luxurious automobile* sometimes is also trying to say that it is a particularly comfortable automobile. So, we also need to take note that:

> Yet no sharp distinction between "luxury" and "comfort" has been generally accepted so far. Many contexts contribute to the conceptual confusion in contemporary linguistic consciousness, in which both words are used without differentiation. The contention, often heard, that "comfort" and "luxury" are for the most part conceptually identical arises even in contexts in which the benefits of "comfort" involve greater effort and value than the benefits of "luxury" (tr.).[6]

In fact, it seems appropriate to carry Mühlmann's conclusions forward systematically: Even if we can observe a linguistic identification of luxury and comfort, this is not semantically significant. For the exaggerated and irrational effort that is rightly called *luxury* simply has nothing to do with comfort, as we can see from an automobile: We may want to say a car is a luxury because it was built by hand, because the motor is extremely complicated and the interior is fitted with silk rugs. These aspects do not increase its comfort, but rather make it impractical, which is, in turn, a loss of comfort. So someone in search of a luxurious object is looking for an exaggeratedly elaborate solution to a practical problem; someone in search of comfort, by contrast, is looking for a solution that is as easy, practical, warm and refreshing as possible. In short: Nothing is luxurious because it is comfortable, or comfortable because it is luxurious.

Here we could take up Kant's argument—already a hint of what is to come—and say: The comfort of something is one form in which we encounter the pleasant in Kant's sense, that is, a simple, positive effect on the senses. The task of distinguishing between comfort and luxury is therefore not simply a lexical matter of distinguishing between two words, but rather raises the same additional issues that Kant raised in

The judgment of luxury **61**

regard to the difference between the pleasant and the beautiful. The goal is to show that the experience of something as comfortable differs fundamentally from the experience of something as luxury. In the second case, people have experiences that no longer make sense as sensual effects; that cannot be reduced to the enjoyment of a sensual pleasure or convenience. This is exactly what the following is about—Thinking of luxury as a phenomenon that stands in the same relationship to comfort as the beautiful does to the pleasant for Kant. In order to describe this in detail, however, it is absolutely necessary to also distinguish clearly between the concepts of luxury and of ostentation. Otherwise, it is easy to get lost.

## Luxury *versus* ostentation

The situation with the concept of ostentation is very like it is with the concept of comfort. Here, too, lies a danger of confusion, and, in this case, with unattractive ideological effects, such as false insinuation. In this case, too, the categorical difference is very easy to define; for here, too, the standard definition suffices. Ostentation is a phenomenon of social *self-presentation*. With ostentation, we are concerned with prestigious objects or status symbols that confer social distinction by means of a symbolic power that is conventionally attributed to them. With this we find ourselves in another discourse, however: Pierre Bourdieu began his study *Distinction: A Social Critique of the Judgment of Taste*, first published in 1979, by describing the principles of social distinction. But these descriptions do not apply to the question of what luxury is. The situation recurs: It may be that the same object is both a luxury good and a status symbol for someone. But that does not mean that the same thing is being said about the object with both words. When something is called ostentatious or pretentious, it means that some braggart—the nice old word has fallen into disuse—is using it as a mark of social distinction. That is the crucial point: The difference between ostentation and luxury is invisible; it is a question of function. The way a thing is used changes constantly. The use of something as symbolic self-presentation says nothing about whether the object was produced with irrational and superfluous effort. Sometimes things seem pretentious even though they have no association with exaggerated effort at all. In this sense, the most banal

**62** The Dadaism of possession

T-shirt with a certain brand works as a pretentious status symbol, ostentatious despite involving no exaggerated effort. Even things deliberately made without a noticeable, to say nothing of an irrational, level of effort can take over a symbolic function and stand for—if not actually constitute—membership in a class or group, and this very thing marks a fundamental difference between ostentation and luxury: The symbolic power of ostentation depends on the public visibility and use of the possession. Only in the public domain, only by way of a deliberate display, does something become ostentatious. This dependence on an onlooker does not apply to luxury, for exaggeration and extravagance can be practiced in private as well. Think of a splendid private garden with tropical plants, or a private library with a collection that extends far beyond the needs of its sole user, it is actually irritating that an interested reader has no access to it. Another example would be hours of bathing in which litres of exquisite scents are wasted. In these cases it would not make sense to speak of ostentation, and that shows that the concepts of luxury and of pretentiousness have fundamentally different contents.

Ostentation is, as discussed, associated with a public, symbolic self-presentation, which, however, does not in turn mean that every symbolic self-presentation is *eo ipso* ostentation. Ostentation is a special case among the various forms of self-presentation by means of consumption, as Wolfgang Ullrich worked out in his study *Habenwollen* [Wanting to Have] of 2006. There, ostentation is an instrument of social self-presentation that is, on the one hand, a symbolic one with a long history, but, on the other hand, an exceptionally awkward one that can transmit only one single content, which states: *The owner has the power to buy.* That is, ostentation is not capable of a subtle presentation of an individual personality through consumer goods—on the contrary: "As status symbols, consumer goods in the past had only limited powers of portrayal. They might disclose someone's wealth and social standing, but not his political views or what his temperament was like" (tr.).[7] For the question of luxury, this means that luxury is always an effort that exceeds the necessary; this exaggerated effort can be used to show off, to symbolize purchasing power and good credit, because an exaggerated effort is, not always, but often, expensive. But what is the case for all symbols is also the case for ostentation: A symbol is a symbol because someone is using it as one.

The judgment of luxury   **63**

It isn't necessarily used in this way; it is contingent; it can fail to happen. No one is obliged to use and view an object as a symbol, even if it has often or ordinarily served as one. Even something that was produced explicitly as a symbol need not be used as a symbol by the possessor, and need not be used as a symbol at all times either.

Here we can draw a clear parallel with the phenomenological position within image theory. Phenomenologists take the view that not every sign is an image, and not every image is used as a sign. Images can be signs if they are used as such; images need not be signs, however, for they need not be used as signs. In particular, it cannot be said that something becomes an image because it is used as a sign. That means that the phenomenological approach to the description of luxury, like the phenomenological approach to the description of the image, refutes the prejudice equally well established in both cases, namely, that we are concerned with symbolic phenomena in both cases: It refutes the contention, that is, that every image is a sign and that every luxury is ostentatious. Because this is in doubt, neither the question of what luxury is nor the question of what an image is can, from a phenomenological standpoint, be answered by means of semiotics or symbol theory. One has only to substitute *luxury* for the expression *image* and *ostentation* for *sign* in the statement discussed above to have the basic idea of a phenomenology of luxury: Not every ostentatious object is a luxury, and not every luxury good is used ostentatiously. Luxury goods can be ostentatious if they are used as such; luxury goods need not be ostentatious, for they need not be used as such. It is clear how analogous the interests of a phenomenology of the image are to those of a phenomenology of luxury.

The distinction in content between luxury and ostentation is of central importance for avoiding false associations as well as crude misunderstandings. In turning to luxury, understood as a genuine form of aesthetic experience, the thought was that in this way one might show that in luxury, human beings find an anthropologically relevant pregnant moment, that is, an experience of feeling themselves existentially human, and that they do so not exclusively, but especially when they live in a utilitarian society. The guiding idea of the phenomenological description is that through luxury, it is possible to have the aesthetic experiences that Schiller finds in *play*, Heidegger in *anxiety* and in *boredom*, and Jünger in *battle* and *intoxication*. But thinking of

**64** The Dadaism of possession

ostentation without distinguishing it from luxury—erroneously, perhaps for moral or ideological reasons—not only interferes with the effort to define an aesthetic phenomenon, but also produces completely misleading theses that hardly anyone would be likely to support.

Hermeneutically, the case is clear: A person can only understand a text if he does not want to misunderstand it. But luxury seems to be such a socially exhausting topic that it may be necessary to explicitly state what, for hermeneutic reasons, must be the case. If luxury is falsely identified with pretentiousness and ostentation, the sentence *A person experiences luxury only when he is human in the full sense of the word, and he is only entirely human when he is experiencing luxury* becomes completely cynical nonsense; so, we should not suppose that anyone would take such a silly idea seriously.

Reflections on luxury as an aesthetic phenomenon are made on linguistically thorny ground. We are confronted by a curious problem of a sort we are unlikely to find again. The same statements have almost diametrically opposed social connotations and associations, depending on whether luxury is identified with ostentation or the two are clearly distinguished. If—for whatever reasons—one thinks automatically of ostentation in connection with luxury, statements that present genuine, socially emancipatory ideas can paradoxically sound like the decadent anthropology of the affluent. The exact opposite is the case, however, the moment a strict division is maintained between *aesthetic experience of self through luxury* and *symbolic self-presentation through ostentation*. Luxury comes into being through private experience, and pretentiousness comes into being through public conventions. We are dealing with effects that run in opposite directions: From the outside in, and from the inside out. At one point the concern is with inner experience and at another with external appearances. If we attend to this diametrical opposition, then, and only then, does a perspective open in which the affirmation of luxury as an aesthetic experience—in Schiller's sense and in his tradition—can move toward a description of an experience of autonomy: *A human being defends himself with luxury against the demands of utilitarian rationality exactly when he is human in the full sense of the word, and he is—certainly not only, but also—entirely human when, through luxury, he has the experience of not having been completely controlled by utilitarian rationality.*

## Necessary for something and necessary for someone

The particular strength of Sombart's definition is surely that it does not throw luxury, comfort and ostentation together. Still, the definition does not suffice. It is not even exact, in the end, because there are two possible ways of understanding it. The sentence "luxury is any effort that exceeds what is necessity" can be understood in two ways: The formulation can refer, first, to the effort required to achieve a goal with technical means and the formulation can also refer to an effort that exceeds what is necessary for human beings. Apparently, there is a technical and an anthropological sense. This double sense applies to the concept of the necessary, for there are two ways of speaking about the necessity of something: If something is necessary it can, on the one hand, be *necessary for an entity, that is, for something*, or it can, on the other hand, be *necessary for a person, that is, for someone*—the difference between them is basic and, for the sense of the concept of luxury, explicitly relevant.

When a person speaks about whether something is *necessary for something*, he is judging the efficiency of an entity. It concerns a technical adequacy: *Necessary for something in order for it to function*. What is being considered and judged is a means-to-an-end relationship in which the means that count as necessary are exactly those that must be there in order to reach the goal. Engineers are regularly concerned with the optimization of a technology in this sense, which is to say a reduction of means to those that are necessary for the effort to be as economical, efficient and simple as possible. Engineers on the whole share the view of Friedrich Nietzsche: They do not understand the superfluous as a welcome supplement to the necessary, but rather believe that "the superfluous is the enemy of necessity" (tr.).[8] But would we want therefore to claim that engineers fight against luxury as an enemy in their work? That would miss the point. Because their decisions regarding necessity occur exclusively within a technical or economic discourse that is defined by an instrumental logic. The outdated oil heating is irrational in this sense: It is not fit for purpose.

In a discussion about something that is *not necessary for a human being*, however, we find ourselves in a completely different kind of conversation: In an anthropological discourse. This is about what a human being must have. What do human beings need? This discourse is not controlled by instrumental logic, but by cultural ideas, especially

**66** The Dadaism of possession

by convictions, opinions and theories about what human beings are and what they reasonably or even essentially must have in life. Many would certainly say that a 600-square-meter single home in central London with a pool and helicopter landing pad would be sheer luxury, even if the heating had the best energy ratings and the whole house was ecologically up-to-date. What is being said is, rather: Such homes are not suited to human beings because they are not necessary for a good, meaningful life—and may actually present obstacles to a good, meaningful life. For in a case of this kind, the decision regarding necessity does not rest on a perfection of technique, but on human beings as the occupants of such objects, and this decision—in turn critical for the argument to come—concerns not a specific person, but human beings as human beings and their genuine requirements: A designation luxury is therefore necessarily based on an anthropological view of a good life. The standard for this decision is the form of life that is apparently *right* for human beings, to which the possession of luxury does not conform.

## A form of life at the middle level

The concept of a form of life can help to describe more exactly what sort of phenomenon is being tested and overstepped by luxury: Goods are described as luxurious if, by means of extravagance, they transgress by disavowing the form of life that is considered right. This human form of life—Rahel Jaeggi was able to pin it down exactly in her *Kritik von Lebensformen* [Critique of Forms of Life] of 2014—presents a curious "'middle ground' between prohibition and whatever an individual may prefer" (tr.).[9] The concept of luxury applies to this very middle ground: For that which is designated luxury is not so inappropriate as to be morally repugnant or legally prohibited—something absolutely prohibited would not be a luxury. With respect to the example, it is not against the law to possess a 600-square-meter flat in London. The very person who, for whatever reasons, considers it wrong, who thinks that such a possession should be prohibited, is one who, for that very reason, should not designate it a luxury, but rather a moral transgression, a crime, an offence or simply as evil. For if he were to speak of luxury, he would be turning something he himself wants to see prohibited into a form of life that is morally or legally entirely possible, if not preferable.

The judgment of luxury **67**

It becomes clear with respect to gross criminality. Imagine someone calling the possession of slaves a luxury. This statement is as cynical and immoral as it is exact, because the concept of luxury refers to a departure from a certain form of life only and does not imply malfeasance or criminality. This is not to say, however, that taking something to be a luxury therefore falls into the category of individual preference and, so, moral irrelevance. For, in fact, more is meant by a negative charge of luxury than that someone personally doesn't like something. This is about a claim in principle, like the answer to the question of whether an apartment should have white walls or patterned carpets. That is the middle ground and the critical point: Although the patterns on the carpets and the 600-square-meters are equally unnecessary for living, the question about the pattern does not concern what is anthropologically appropriate, only individual preference—which is the reason patterns and ornaments do not ordinarily qualify as luxury, despite being unnecessary and superfluous. For luxury, through an excess of effort, oversteps a notion of what is appropriate in principle, without this transgression coming into conflict with the law.

In short: The person who regards the apartment in London as luxury means it in principle. He means that it is exaggerated, excessive, extravagant, inappropriate and unreasonable for *any human being* to live in such a flat. He is relating the flat to an idea of actual human beings and about the right way for them to live. One who designates something as luxury does so ostensibly knowing how people should live, and in fact knowing this even better and more precisely than moral prohibitions or legal regulations establish as possible ways of living. Only, this means that if someone should try to ground his view of the status of something as luxury, he would basically have to explain his idea of human beings, their actual requirements; he would have to set out an essential or ideal view of humanity. The foundation of this idea would come down to a more or less known anthropological argument or description of human beings. Or, perhaps it would only amount to so many declarations that feed, knowingly or unknowingly, on various discourses and intellectual traditions: On ethical, political, religious, aesthetic, economic, medial, historical, philosophical, cultural or ideological views and theories.

It is worth noting that this central idea can also be found in Edward Johns Urwick's book *Luxury and Waste of Life* of 1908—although in a

**68** The Dadaism of possession

very offhand way, as hardly more than an incidental remark that the author himself did not find important. Still, it does not change the fact that one short sentence about judgments of luxury—in an otherwise philosophically uninteresting book—is exceptionally apt: "In every case an appeal is made to a theory of life."[10] That is, in order for something to be a luxury, there must be a theory of human beings that permits effort to be defined as inappropriate. The reverse is also the case, however: For someone advancing a theory or a picture of human beings in which this is not possible, there can be no luxury. Jean-Paul Sartre is a good example of it.

Hardly any other philosopher defends, as Sartre does, the extreme view that human beings have no essential characteristic except their freedom. There is no other mark of human authenticity. For existentialists, the idea of an essential or true human nature is an obsolete myth, used only for purposes of oppression. That means that existentialists cannot go too far. Because individual human beings cannot be considered realizations of something essential, nothing in the world can qualify as luxury. There is no senseless waste for existentialists, to say nothing of a Dadaism of possession. A person may really extend himself, he may do exactly as he pleases, lie on yachts on the Côte d'Azur as long as he likes or have as many grand apartments in Paris, Sartre's idea of an appropriate lifestyle cannot be overstepped or invalidated because he wants to abolish every idea of the necessary and appropriate as disingenuous self-deception, and this with a shocking implication, as well, that even supplies like bread and water are— at least for the early Sartre of *Being and Nothingness* of 1943—only apparently necessary for many people because they mistakenly argue using a premise that comes from a "spirit of worthiness" and "insincerity": "because it is *necessary* to live."[11] But Sartre does not accept this premise. On the contrary: Why must a person actually live? According to Sartre there is nothing essential about a human being that requires that he live. A human being does not have to but, at most, decides to live. The only thing a human being has to be is free: "a human being is condemned to be free."[12] To this extent a living person is, for Sartre, always already doing something that is not necessary for human beings. For an existentialist there is, in fact, no luxury in life. Instead, all of life is a luxury he could do without.

## The two levels of the judgment of luxury

If we consider talk about luxury with the distinctions between *necessary for some purpose* and *necessary for human beings* in the background, we notice a curious semantic structure that may be unique to the concept of luxury. It involves traffic in double meanings. What is remarkable is not that Sombart's sentence has a double meaning—that is the case for many sentences. The sentence *Luxury is any effort that exceeds what is necessary* means, as noted, first, *luxury is any effort that exceeds what is necessary for something*, and second, *luxury is any effort that exceeds what is necessary for someone*. The salient point is that neither of these sentences—or to put it another way, neither of the two meanings of Sombart's sentence *on its own*—is accurate and apt as a definition of luxury.

The example of the outdated heating system shows that the sentence *luxury is any effort that exceeds the necessary for something* is inadequate. We can show that the sentence *luxury is any effort that exceeds the necessary for someone*, too, is inadequate for an apt definition with the example of a compulsive hoarder. For if we direct the question about necessity for someone to all kinds of things rather than only toward things that have taken an excessive amount of time and trouble to make, then the completely rubbish-filled home of a hoarder would be an instance of opulent luxury. In the end it is full of stuff most people would consider superfluous and unnecessary for anyone.

Luxury can be defined neither solely with a technical *necessity for something* nor solely with an anthropological *necessity for someone*, but only by means of a decision in which both kinds of necessity interact and are taken into consideration. The following suggestion shows how such an interplay of criteria might look: The first meaning of Sombart's definition can be understood as defining the necessary characteristic of luxury and the second meaning as defining a sufficient characteristic. Then the definition goes: Luxury is any effort that exceeds both what is technically necessary for something and what is anthropologically necessary for someone. With this we have a specific decision structure with a two-part order for a judgment of luxury. With the concept of luxury, we consider the necessity of something that is not necessary. To put it more exactly: We consider the human necessity of technical excess, material waste and inefficiency due to

**70** The Dadaism of possession

exaggeration. If we take the view that something is luxury, we are taking something *unnecessary to not be necessary*. This is not a rare occurrence. It is not only in extreme situations that a decision about instrumental-rational necessity is made on the basis of whether it is necessary for humans. Think of a tuxedo as evening dress or even of just a simple tie. A person who finds this appropriate, perhaps even necessary in the situation, ordinarily does not defend it as practical, functional clothing; he would not describe it as luxury either, but resorts to aesthetic, social, historical and cultural ideas about people that make it appear to be necessary, or at least appropriate, to take the trouble to wear such clothing on this occasion—even when it is impractical. In such situations, the issue is not an estimate of the effort and the thing's fitness for purpose, but a consideration of whether people in their respective cultural, historical and financial situations need this unnecessary thing or this unnecessary effort. This is the reason an anthropological or ideological view is always inherent in a judgment of luxury. Some who perhaps think that opera houses are luxuries, doubt that unpractical, uneconomical, lavish opera productions are necessary for humans—which can be the expression of various views of humanity. Among them is the view that human beings, before they do anything else, should make sure that as many people as possible in this world can live well. In light of widespread misery in the world, the opulence of opera houses appears to be an unreasonable and irrational waste, that is, a luxury. For it is not controversial: What is a practical, utilitarian opera? Someone who understands people as beings that are always in need of fresh reflection on themselves and their human situation—including the world's misery—through the medium of art will consider opera to be an essential cultural possession, if not a factor in actually sustaining life.

In short, the deconstruction shows that the judgment of luxury is a judgment on two levels, in which a judgment and a meta-judgment are merged. In the judgment as well as in the meta-judgment a necessity is under consideration—although a different one in each case. The point of entry and the basis for this judgment of luxury is a decision about the technical, utilitarian aspect of something; in this way a necessary characteristic is defined—reasonable luxury is a contradiction. The only things that can be luxuries are things a utilitarian logic considers irrational, exaggerated, baroque, impractical, unreasonable,

The judgment of luxury **71**

extravagant, inefficient, inappropriate and uneconomical. Yet, not everything that finds itself on this list is a luxury on those grounds alone. This thing must further overstep notions of what is necessary for human beings. What is technically unnecessary is considered once again in the meta-judgment with regard to whether it is necessary for human beings in a particular situation. A statement such as *that is luxury for me* sounds self-contradictory, much as *that is true for me* does, or, for Kant, the statement *that is beautiful for me*. However, someone who says *the food is delicious for me* might have spared himself the *for me*, for to say something is delicious is a sense judgment that is valid *a priori* only *for me*. And yet—and this is a key point—a view of what human beings really need and what is extravagant and superfluous under concrete social conditions depends on an anthropological understanding of human beings. People have decidedly different ideas in this respect—as we can see from more than opera houses alone. But despite this diversity and multiplicity of implicit and explicit anthropological views, there is a rational basis. Forms of life can be critiqued. It is very definitely possible to disagree about the different answers to the question of how a person should live authentically, truly and really well. For this reason, a categorical assertion of luxury is different from an ordinary subjective opinion.

## The judgment of luxury's claim to generality

The best-known examples of exclusively subjective judgments are such statements as: *The noodles are delicious, the water is pleasantly warm.* Kant (1789) calls these judgments "judgments of sense" in the *Critique of Judgment*. They are exclusively private judgments, and their validity cannot be imposed on or demonstrated to others by means of arguments. That singles these judgments out: They do not imply any truth for others. It is simply foolish and pointless to disagree about whether the water is pleasantly warm or a little cool: For one person it is this way, for another that way. The sense judgment merely acknowledges subjective sensitivities.

Since the situation with luxury is known to be similar—something is luxury for one person that is perfectly normal for another—this apparent similarity could be misunderstood as evidence that judgments of luxury, too, are subjective private judgments, just like Kant's sense

**72** The Dadaism of possession

judgments. But the situation is fundamentally different: In a judgment of luxury we are dealing with a type of judgment that rather recalls, in its formal qualities, Kant's judgments of taste. The judgment of taste—for example *the garden is beautiful*—has an intermediate formal position for Kant. It is, on the one hand, aesthetic, like a sense judgment, that is, the effect something has on the observer plays a part in this judgment: Does it produce pleasure or aversion? On the other hand, however, the judgment of taste is constructed grammatically exactly like a judgment of knowledge that gives a characteristic of something—for example, *the garden is dry*. That is, although grammatically speaking the judgment of taste credits the beautiful thing with being beautiful, beauty is not a characteristic of this beautiful thing. For the judgment of taste and the sense judgment are, for Kant, both of the type *estimation*; these do not establish the characteristic of a thing, but rather estimate a thing according to an external standard. For Kant, this standard is the effect on the subject: The observer's or consumer's sense of pleasure or of aversion, both in the case of the estimation of whether something is beautiful or of whether something is pleasant.

But Kant believed that he had further shown, in his *Critique of Judgment*, that the subjective estimation of beauty—like a judgment of knowledge—has a claim to generality. Unlike a sense judgment, a judgment of taste demands something: It is formulated with a claim to generality. A true judgment of taste must have the support of others, just as others must agree with a true judgment of knowledge. From this combination comes a specific type of judgment characterized by its intermediate position: The judgment of taste is, on the one hand, an aesthetic judgment of subjective pleasure or aversion, but is, on the other hand, bound up with the obligations of a claim to generality.

In order to avoid misunderstandings, this is not about the contents of the judgments, but about the formally intermediate position. We are therefore not concerned about the beauty of many luxury goods, or about many beautiful things also being considered luxuries. The structural affinity has to do with a characteristic of both judgments. In this respect, a judgment of luxury is comparable with a judgment of taste in Kant's sense, for neither the judgment of luxury nor the judgment of taste is either a judgment of sense or a judgment of knowledge. In the cases of both the judgment of luxury and the judgment

The judgment of luxury **73**

of taste, there is a partial overlap between a judgment of sense and a judgment of knowledge.

The judgment of luxury is an estimation, like a judgment of taste or a sense judgment; an estimate is given with respect to a standard—in the one case this standard is a sense of pleasure or aversion, in the other it is necessity in two senses. The estimation-character of these judgments leads to a noteworthy parallel. Say someone is standing in front of a closed door and says: *In the room behind the door there are pleasant, beautiful and luxurious things.* Nothing has been said here about how the things behind the door look or what other qualities they have. None of the three terms describe anything about the way the things in the room are made. That applies to any estimation. From a mark of *adequate* on a piece of schoolwork one knows nothing about the content of the work. And that is exactly what distinguishes a sense-, taste- or luxury-judgment from a knowledge judgment. For with the knowledge judgment something is said about the thing. If someone standing in front of the closed door hears that there is a bicycle behind it, he knows by means of this statement how one of the things in the room looks—at least he knows which characteristics it must have if the statement *that is a bicycle* is true.

The next point is more critical. If the parallels between judgments of taste in Kant's sense and the judgment of luxury are to be pushed further, both would have to claim general validity, for this very claim would then be what both judgments had in common with the judgment of knowledge. And this claim to generality is actually what puts both judgments in a formally intermediate position. Judgments of taste and judgments of luxury are both estimations with a claim to general validity. Both make the same demand of other people. For a judgment of luxury implies, much as a judgment of taste does, a subtle claim to general validity. But no elaborate transcendental argument is needed to support it, as is the case for Kant and the judgment of taste. (Whether he actually succeeded in providing a transcendental proof is another question, the answer to which is not significant for the formal analogy between the judgment of taste and the judgment of luxury.) A judgment of luxury is happily much clearer in this respect. A luxury judgment's claim to general validity requires just one explanation, which is an account of what is meant when something is defined as luxury. Whoever says that something is a luxury is *always*

**74** The Dadaism of possession

*also* saying that he himself does not need this thing—but that is *never all* he is saying. In making a judgment of luxury he is further claiming that something is superfluous, as such, for anyone. For the one making it, an estimate of something as luxury indicates a conflict between a particular view of humanity and a reality that challenges it. A claim to general validity raised by means of a judgment of luxury is therefore always justified and persuasive to the extent that the notion of humanity implicit in the judgment is justified and persuasive. The two validities are directly proportional: A statement about luxury is true or false to the extent its implied understanding of humanity is true or false—and that is absolutely remarkable. For the concept of luxury's inherent dependence on an understanding of what it is like to be a human being is a rare phenomenon from a linguistic standpoint. There may be just one relational concept that is comparable in this respect: The concept of the healthy.

## Luxury and the concept of the healthy

The common ground between statements such as *meat is healthy* and *meat is a luxury* is straightforward: In both cases the judgments are of a type estimation that someone can make only if he has a view of *what human beings need in order to live*. For an estimation is always made using a criterion. In the case of the healthy, as in that of luxury, we are concerned with a standard that is not considered valid exclusively for oneself. It is the same for smoking: We would vehemently oppose someone who was asserting in all seriousness that for him, personally, smoking is healthy, even though he was claiming it only for himself. That is the common ground. In both cases, the estimation of whether something is healthy or whether something is a luxury rests on an implicit view of humanity, which does not mean that we would always agree about whether the underlying understanding of humanity in any one specific case is persuasive. Differences in answers to the question of what a human being is and what is necessary, right and important for him are known to lead, in specific cases, to sharply divergent estimations of what is healthy and unhealthy, what is luxury and what isn't.

But as divergent as medical, anthropological and cultural understandings of human beings may be, they are discussable in principle.

The judgment of luxury **75**

Efforts can be made to support them with arguments. Views that contradict one's own may be refuted and criticized. This is the decisive correlation. To the same extent that an understanding of human beings is persuasive for someone—for whatever reasons—a statement about whether something is healthy or is a luxury, that relies on this understanding, will be persuasive as well. With this, we can see an analytical relationship between the concepts of luxury and health: A view of the question "What is healthy?" necessarily implies a view of the question of *what is not a luxury*. Caution is advisable here, however, for that does not mean, as one might mistakenly conclude, that a view of *what is healthy* would also necessarily imply *what luxury is*. There is only one conceptual-analytical implication for a negation! An example can make this clearer: A person who is convinced that it is healthy to drink two litres of water every day must necessarily agree that the possession of two litres of water is *not a luxury*. A person who is convinced that eating meat is unnecessary and superfluous is not automatically also saying that meat is a luxury, although he has fulfilled the necessary conditions to hold this view.

The concepts *luxurious* and *healthy* are similar in that both, to the same extent, make an estimation on the basis of an understanding of human beings. Still, we should not overlook the difference. If an effort is considered inadequate to satisfy an understanding of what a person needs to be healthy, it is always also an explicitly negative evaluation of this thing, situation or form of life. Only a cynical blockhead would ask, out of interest, with respect to a catastrophic famine: *And what value can we ascribe to this catastrophe?* So we can say: The judgment of an effort as insufficient to achieve what is necessary is always, in the very performance of the speech act, an explicitly negative evaluation of the shortcoming. The linguistic designation of something as unhealthy alone evaluates that thing negatively. That is: An estimation as healthy is always an evaluation as well. Or to put it another way: *Healthy* is a deontological concept, and that sets it apart from the concept of luxury. The estimation of something as *effort that willfully and impractically exceeds what is necessary* by no means instantly and automatically pronounces an evaluation—either a negative or a positive one. We should keep this in mind particularly in light of the way the concept of luxury is frequently used in the same way that the concept of the unhealthy is, that is to say,

**76** The Dadaism of possession

as if it automatically implied a negative evaluation, sometimes even as if it were diagnosing an illness.

## Luxury judgments and evaluations

There is a danger of confusion: On the one hand, judgments of luxury are always estimations, and, on the other hand, evaluations, too, are always estimations. It would therefore be easy to think that judgments of luxury, too, are evaluations—but this is not the case. For in an evaluation the decision concerns whether something is as this thing *should be* according to a criterion. In an evaluation the criterion specifies a desirable ideal, although this by no means applies to every use of every standard. Someone measuring a table with a yardstick is using a standard too, but without evaluating the table in the process. Unlike the use of the yardstick as a standard, an evaluation amounts to a comparison between an "is" condition and a "should be" condition. This "should be" condition cannot be derived from the "is" condition, but must rather be brought in from outside as an evaluation criterion and applied to the "is" condition. If a positive evaluation is reached, this means that something can be defined as admirable, as good, as the desirable realization of an idea of something ideal or normal—or at least as something that is as it should be.

This is not the case for a judgment of luxury. From the contention that a visit to a sauna is a luxury, we can tell that the speaker finds saunas extravagant, and so superfluous for human beings. But this does not necessarily mean a negative evaluation at all. Luxury may be respected and is respected by quite a few. In the statement, *that is luxury*, something is definitely being compared with something else—namely the thing under consideration with some notion of what is necessary. But there is no decision about whether the transgression should be considered positive or negative. We may just as well welcome as reject the idea that human beings should behave in rational, reasonable, conventional, appropriate and reliably safe ways. Luxury contradicts means-to-an-end thinking—negative and positive evaluations of this are always equally possible. When someone confirms, *That is luxury!*, it is always still meaningful to ask: *And how do you like it?*

This means, in sum, that taking the level of evaluation into account, views about luxury can diverge and be discussed on three

The judgment of luxury    **77**

levels, and in fact with rational grounds for each one: *First*, around the question of whether something is technically efficient, *second*, with respect to whether this something is inappropriately exaggerated for human beings, and *third*, in evaluating whether this kind of excess is considered valuable or not. However one may stand with respect to a designation of something as luxury, whenever there is doubt about the justification it is helpful to note the level where the reflections have taken place. It is particularly helpful in keeping the *luxury estimation* from being quietly confused with the *luxury evaluation*. For it is not at all unusual to observe the concept of luxury being used as a category of value in a given situation, so that the designation alone is enough to elliptically pronounce an evaluation. A vacationer in the South Seas, raving about the luxury of his exclusive journey and describing it explicitly as luxury, will probably have no further need to explain that what he means here by luxury is something positive. Conversely, a pastor hardly needs to explain that in his sermon on luxury in a capitalistic world, he is referring to a social problem, if not an actual evil. We can go further and say: The ambivalence of luxury in the modern world, a concept with equally vehement defenders and detractors, can be traced into everyday language. We are dealing with an expression that can be used elliptically as a term of abuse or also as a compliment, depending on context. This seems to be especially clear when luxury appears in a combination of words as a prefix. Mention of a luxury hotel in an advertisement is intended to be positive *a priori*, whereas a hard-core Rousseau devotee uses the concept of luxury tendentiously, as if he were diagnosing an illness. But these associations are ideologically conditioned in both cases; the principle applies when something is determined to be inefficient, superfluous and unnecessary for human beings, then this something can be evaluated, after the decision is made, as either positive or negative. For not every estimation of something as superfluous has to be an evaluation.

## Luxury: a product of interpretation?

The interim result seems to be: Luxury is the product of an interpretation of something technically not necessary, as something unnecessary for human beings, which then, in a given situation, is interpreted further as good or bad. We could also say: Reflections on the judgment

**78** The Dadaism of possession

of luxury give philosophical interpretationism a footing. If something is to be called luxury solely on the basis of an *estimation*, this means, at the same time, that it is called luxury solely on the basis of an *interpretation*—for it is clear that estimations are interpretations after all: They read and define *something as something*. Whether an object is a luxury depends, accordingly, solely on whether one interprets it as luxury— and obviously not every object in every situation will be interpreted by everyone as luxury. No one would claim such a thing. So the thesis states: For every object, it is possible to think of people in situations that could interpret the object as luxury on good grounds. Interpretationism even seems to speak to changing ideas about what specific things qualify as luxury at what times. Ideas about what luxury is change as a result of constant changes in the usual and normal possibilities in a society. This is the reason a luxury object seems an almost exemplary verification of what interpretationists claim for all objects in the world: Everything that is, is that which it is on the basis of interpretation. There are no facts independent of interpretation. Rather, that which is becomes what it is through an interpretive perception and an interpreting language. The concept of social construction, too, seems as appropriate to luxury as it is to money, which is not surprising if every construction is a form of interpretation. That is: If there were no society that allowed money or luxury to exist, then there would be no money or luxury. For there is agreement on this point: Money is a product of social interpretation because something is money only if, and as long as, there is a society constructing money through its interpretations.

However one may view the extreme claim to generality made by interpretationism or constructivism as philosophical positions, these views seem at first glance to be in accord with the theme of luxury, including the logical conclusion: It is not the object that determines whether it is a luxurious object through its specific material or physical qualities, but rather an interpretation as luxury that is brought to the object. Only the critical question is: Is this interpretation in language decisive in itself? Are luxury goods—like money—social constructs? If that were the case, nothing could be luxury unless a society made it possible to interpret and so to describe this something in this way. It concerns the claim of exclusivity. For interpretationism does not claim that acts of interpretation are involved in the estimation of something as

The judgment of luxury **79**

luxury. Who would doubt this banal thesis? Rather, it concerns the philosophically challenging thesis that whether something is luxury depends entirely on acts of speech and interpretation alone.

This thesis has far-reaching consequences. One of them is: The relation between a person and a luxury object is a relation constituted exclusively through an act of interpretation. That means specifically that if two people interpret the same object as luxury, they would have a connection to this object that at least could no longer be distinguished linguistically. The object would be luxury to the same extent for both because both interpret this thing as luxury to the same degree. In other respects, they might go on to perceive this object differently; one might find it beautiful and the other might interpret it as kitschy instead. But with respect to the question as to whether the object is luxury for the person in question, they would have the same interpretation and so in this respect the same internal relation to the object. The conclusion is absurd and far removed from the unspoken common assumption about luxury that succeeds best in grasping the very point on which interpretationism fails. This is the phenomenon of the experience of luxury.

## The limits of interpretationism

Imagine a person working in a luxury hotel who perhaps does not have the best job there. This woman or this man spends more time in the splendid rooms of this hotel than the guests do, as they constantly come and go. Since he has been working in the hotel for years, usually from morning to evening, one could even say that he spends a good part of his life there. Imagine further that this person thinks, as in fact all the employees do, that the hotel in question is not practical, efficient, comfortable accommodation, but rather that for everything and nothing—wherever you look, wherever you go—far more fuss is made than is necessary. The hotel employee furthermore has a very clear view of the splendor and the extravagance he sees in the hotel day in and day out. He is pleased that there are so many guests that pay for it and so ensure his employment. But he also thinks that people as people don't need such a hotel. On the contrary, he actually finds the hotel completely superfluous and thinks that the money could be spent to far better effect. He has his own ideas about this. In

**80** The Dadaism of possession

short, he has good grounds for concluding that the hotel is a bombastic luxury with no ifs or buts—and yet could anyone seriously claim that *the personnel in a luxury hotel live in luxury?* Hardly! It would actually be arrogant and demeaning of someone to speak of the luxurious life of hotel employees.

The crucial point in this example seems to be the following: It shows us something that is often the case in philosophy—that which is so evident on the one hand is, on the other hand, difficult to grasp and to describe. The hotel personnel and the guests have *different intentional relationships* to the same luxury, even if both spend time in the same spaces, and the spaces look the same to both—and we are concerned with precisely this difference in the way something is intentionally given for people, that is, with a genuinely phenomenological issue. The aesthetic differences are not based on a difference in visibility, for the same things are seen by the guests and by the personnel—and still there is an aesthetic difference in the manner in which the same things are things for someone. This difference does not, remarkably, concern the beauty of the things seen. In fact, we could say that the personnel spend time in beautiful spaces. That is exactly the point: The contemplation of beauty quickly drifts into aesthetic and asocial statements about the world. At least since Kant, both guests and personnel have to approach the things in the hotel in an equally disinterested way in order to then be able to experience their beauty equally. By contrast, the judgment of whether something is luxury is not based on such a cold, distanced contemplation that dissolves conscious social differences. And so it is, guests and personnel cannot experience the hotel's luxury to the same extent.

This phenomenal and aesthetic difference in the kind of experience, the way something is for someone, needs to be grasped categorically—and this is exactly where interpretationism reaches its limit. The example of personnel in a luxury hotel is an instance of a phenomenal difference that cannot be grasped as long as luxury is held to be exclusively a culturally variable product of interpretation. The guests and the personnel of the hotel are actually in complete agreement about their interpretation or estimation of the hotel. In this respect they are not different—the hotel is luxury. But guests and personnel do not have the same intentional relationship to the hotel they call luxurious. To entertain a concept of luxury that could conclude that they do, to therefore fail to distinguish

The judgment of luxury  **81**

phenomenally between them in their intentional relationship to something that counts as luxury, would be misleadingly reductive of the relationship between people and luxury. A further differentiation is therefore needed that recognizes the way people can have different intentional relationships to extravagant and elaborate things, a differentiation that cannot be grasped with an interpretationistic concept of luxury. This is to say that exaggerated and elaborate things may be given to different people in subjectively and phenomenologically different ways, even if there is agreement that the things are exaggerated and elaborate. And the good thing is that this difference can be pinpointed quite easily. Both—the guests and the employees—*interpret* the hotel linguistically as luxury to the same extent but *experience* this luxury in completely different ways.

For human beings, luxury is not merely a construct of linguistic interpretation, it is also an experience. The crucial insight, which states that *the experience of something extends beyond identifying it with a concept*, cannot be gained merely by looking at luxury. If luxury were not bound up with a specific form of aesthetic experience of something we would have to accept the interpretationist interpretation of luxury. But luxury—by contrast to ostentation—is a product of neither social nor linguistic interpretation. It is rather the object of a particular experience. Banal as the evidence may sound, it is that important for philosophical description. The phenomenological content—the way the visible world of luxury hotels is experienced—is phenomenally different for people with power over the hotel, that is, for the guests, and for those without such power, that is, for the personnel. For the guests, the relationship to a luxury object is associated with an individual experience of luxury that the personnel cannot have. This difference in experience or involvement can be introduced as the basis for something being a luxury for someone at all. For the guests, luxury is an experienced phenomenon of presence in which they physically participate. But the personnel see only the luxury of others. They look past it, so to speak, without being in it. Anyone who does no more than perceive what luxury can be, remains an observer. Observation alone does not constitute an experience of luxury. The observed things are rather seen as what luxury could be—but, for the one looking, not what luxury is.

With this, the answer to the question "What is luxury?" has reached a point where one mark of luxury can be established that cannot be reached by analyzing language or judgment. A supplementary phenomenological

**82** The Dadaism of possession

description is therefore needed, that is, a description of the way luxury is experienced in the first person singular. In this way we come to the idea of luxury as a specific form of *aesthetic experience*. To put it more exactly, an object becomes a luxury object for someone by means of a linguistic interpretation, construction or estimation, but not by such means alone, there must always also be an aesthetic experience that goes with it. The condition that must be added to a purely external, linguistic interpretation as luxury, in order for something to be a luxury for a person, is a *particular experience*, an *experience sui generis*. For something only becomes a luxury for someone by having an exceptional effect, based on a recipient's particular attitude toward an *effort that exceeds what is necessary*. Someone who does not have this experience perhaps knows which things are typically interpreted as luxury; however, he does not know what it is like to be the possessor of things associated with superfluous effort. This is not to refute the objective definition of luxury as *any effort that exceeds not only what is necessary for something, but also what is necessary for someone*. Although it is not sufficient, this definition remains persuasive as the first step. The interpretation of something as *an effort that exceeds not only what is necessary for something, but also what is necessary for someone* is the necessary condition for something to be luxury. But to this necessary condition, another, sufficient one must be added in order for it to be luxury. This sufficient condition is an experience brought about by an object that fulfills the necessary conditions. That is, only through his own, particular experience of the thing that has been interpreted in this way can the possibility of this thing being a luxury for someone be realized. One could also say, the situation with luxury is like it is with an illness.

## Having an illness and having luxury

For illnesses too, an outsider can linguistically decide whether someone has an illness. He can use the criteria that indicate an illness; he then makes accurate statements—a doctor often much better than the patient himself. But the patient—not the doctor—knows what it is like to have this illness. There is an experiential dimension to being ill. The relationship between an illness and the one who has it cannot, in turn, be transposed into a purely linguistic, interpretive decision about this relationship, just as it cannot be for luxury; this does not cast any doubt on a doctor's ability to *also* identify an illness accurately

The judgment of luxury **83**

in an objective way. But an illness is not completely grasped from a linguistic identification, for its reality is also bound up with the experience of a subjective state of mind. Distracted postmodernists may therefore think of illnesses as social or linguistic constructions as much as they like—it doesn't resolve the issue, the evidence being that one can suffer and die from illnesses of which society knows nothing.

The ontological common ground between a luxury object and a disease is that when either of the two exists there is someone there who *has* this object or this disease. Ontologically, diseases are always seen as *the disease for someone—in fact for the one who has it*. And the same holds for luxury: Luxury is seen ontologically as luxury for someone—in fact for the one who has it. The personnel in the luxury hotel have the kind of relation to the luxury in the hotel that the hospital personnel have to the illnesses in the hospital.

And yet there is an enormous difference between *having an illness* and *having a luxury*. For many illnesses, if perhaps not for all, medical diagnostic methods and criteria for decisions do not vary with the situation or the culture. Hardly anyone would accept the thesis that on the basis of a social interpretation, depending on the situation and the culture, anyone can have cholera. For more than a few diseases, a very exact empirical determination can be made of whether someone is suffering from it. In this sense there are objective criteria for the presence of a disease; it is not rare for a blood sample to be enough for a reliable diagnosis. So, it is not difficult to imagine, and it certainly often happens, that someone has an illness without knowing he has it. It is different for luxury! Because having a luxury is necessarily bound up with an experience of the one who has it, it is impossible for someone to have a luxury without knowing it. And that means, to return to the example of the hotel, that the evidence that the personnel in a luxury hotel experience the irrational, exaggerated effort differently from the guests is certainly correct and necessary. But it should not lead to the false assumption that every guest in the hotel automatically actually has the experience of luxury. Just because the conditions of possibility for such an experience are met by an irrational, exaggerated effort, it does not mean that anyone automatically actually has this experience. So we need a more exact phenomenological description of when an object is a luxury for someone.

**84** The Dadaism of possession

## Notes

1 Albert Görland, "Über den Begriff des Luxus: Eine philosophische Kritik," *Kant-Studien* 31 (1926), 45.
2 ibid., 30.
3 Werner Sombart, *Luxury and Capitalism*, trans. W.R. Ditmar (Ann Arbor: University of Michigan Press, 1967 [1913]), 3.
4 Johann Georg Krünitz, *Oeconomische Encyklopädie oder allgemeines System der Land-, Haus- und Staats-Wirtschaft* 1773–1858, Vol. 82 (Berlin: Joachim Pauli, 1801). See under "Luxus," 40.
5 Horst Mühlmann, *Luxus und Komfort. Wortgeschichte und Wortvergleich* (Bonn: Rheinische Friedrich-WilhelmsUniversität, 1975), 302.
6 ibid., 303.
7 Wolfgang Ullrich, *Habenwollen: Wie funktioniert die Konsumkultur?* (Frankfurt/M.: Fischer, 2008 [2006]), 19.
8 Friedrich Nietzsche, "On the Utility and Liability of History for Life," in *Unfashionable Observations*, Vol. 2, trans. Richard T. Gray (Stanford: Stanford University Press, 1995 [1874]), 85.
9 Rahel Jaeggi, *Kritik von Lebensformen* (Berlin: Suhrkamp, 2014), 29.
10 Edward Johns Urwick, *Luxury and Waste of Life* (London: J.M. Dent, 1908), 3.
11 Jean-Paul Sartre, *Being and Nothingness: An Essay on Phenomenological Ontology*, trans. Hazel E. Barnes (London: Routledge, 2003 [1943]), 626.
12 Jean-Paul Sartre, *Existentialism and Humanism*, trans. Philip Mairet (London: Eyre Methuen, 1973 [1946]), 34.

# 4

# LUXURY

## A special aesthetic experience

### When is luxury?

It is generally the case that the same or a very similar object will count as luxury or not at various times and in various contexts. The same object can be experienced as luxury by one person and by another person as the most normal thing in the world. There are tests for illnesses, but no scientific test for luxury, because the existence of luxury is not based on the presence of physical qualities. A jeweller can test whether a necklace is made of real gold, but not whether it is real luxury. That, in turn, is nothing out of the ordinary, but rather a state of affairs familiar from many everyday things. A jeweller is equally unable to test whether the necklace is a souvenir or a gift.

Souvenirs, gifts and luxury goods have two ontological characteristics: First, they are what they are for a certain person at a certain time, and second, no one can tell by looking at them that they are what they are. The same object can be, for someone for a specific time, a souvenir at one moment, a gift at another and a luxury good at still another. We can also observe that an object can cease to be perceived and experienced by this person as a luxury, for example because it has become familiar, although this person continues without reservation to interpret the object as an effort that exceeds both what is necessary for something as well what is necessary for someone. Here, we can once again see that it is not just a social or linguistic interpretation that turns something into a luxury.

**86** The Dadaism of possession

If we take the temporal character of luxury seriously it becomes clear that to approach the project of a description of luxury by way of the classical question "What is luxury?" is already to steer slightly off course. A what-is question directs attention—perhaps not necessarily, but by implication—toward the object as such and evokes an idea that it has essential characteristics that can be defined. But that will not work for luxury, because the essential characteristics of luxury simply do not exist in the material sense. There is no measuring or seeing whether something is luxury. We therefore need to change the perspective. If the phenomenal and temporal character is to be placed at the heart of the description, the ontological what-is question must be replaced in the following way: What does the special experience look like that someone must have when something is a luxury for him? What kind of experience of something justifies calling that thing a luxury?

The philosopher Nelson Goodman found himself confronted with the same problem in a description of art. Artworks cannot be recognized and defined as artworks using visible or measurable characteristics either. An artwork does not show why or whether it is an artwork. For everything we might say about the visible qualities of a readymade in a museum—for example about Andy Warhol's *Brillo Boxes*—could just as well be said about many identical cartons of cleaning products in a supermarket. Goodman therefore assumes that artworks—like luxury goods—are only ever artworks for someone for a time. As a consequence of this insight he suggests, in his well-known essay of the same name from 1977, replacing the question "What is art?" with the question "When is art?" A sensible suggestion! So, following Goodman, on the grounds that the situation is analogous, we should ask about luxury as well: "When is luxury?"

That makes the framework for the investigation of luxury oddly incomprehensible. It is perhaps uncontroversial that philosophers show a heightened interest in just those aesthetic phenomena with distinguishing marks that are not material or visible. In any case, in philosophical aesthetics—perhaps since Kant—there has been a widely shared view that neither the question "What is art?" nor the question "What is beauty?" can be answered simply by defining the qualities of perceptible objects. This is exactly the reason that the two questions have always attracted a great deal of philosophical attention. It seems that so far no one has asked whether the same applies to the answer

A special aesthetic experience **87**

to the question "What is luxury?" whether luxury is, therefore, at least as challenging and intriguing, whether for this reason luxury could or should stand beside beauty and art as a central theme in philosophical aesthetics.

However we frame the question, whether more traditionally as "What is luxury?" or perhaps more precisely as "When is Luxury?" what matters is the answer—and this is: An object is luxury as long as it is the object of a special aesthetic experience. More exactly: An object becomes luxury for the time it is experienced by someone in a special aesthetic way that intensifies his sense of himself as human. So luxury announces itself in the context of someone perceiving something as luxury. What happens next is as follows, the first step is to explain what is special about an aesthetic experience as such, then to describe, in a second step, why luxury constitutes a special form of what is already special in any case—aesthetic experience.

## Features of aesthetic experience I: an operational orientation

The plan may cause concern—to reach back to the concept of aesthetic experience is truly not without difficulties. In many theories of reception aesthetics it is used in ways that are too vague, too varied, too inflationary. But as justifiable as this reservation is, it should not get in the way of seeing that the basic sense of the concept can be defined, especially since this has already been done in exemplary fashion. We can draw on the reflections of Martin Seel—we can speak of aesthetic experience when an ordinary experience is modified in a particular way. An "aesthetic perception, first, assumes a capacity for non-aesthetic perception, and second, represents a modification of these acts of non-aesthetic perception" (tr.).[1] Here, aesthetic perception is achieved when ordinary intentional perception of something—such as the seeing, hearing, feeling, tasting of something becomes, for whatever reasons, extraordinary. This is not to say, however, that every modification of perception leads to an aesthetic perception. What is different with respect to ordinary experience is, first, that aesthetic experience is *operationally oriented* and second, that it is *self-referential*.

**88** The Dadaism of possession

The first feature defines the *necessary characteristic* of an aesthetic experience. This condition, the operational orientation toward perception as such, is met when the perceiving person takes a particular attitude with respect to his own perception. He must behave really unnaturally, for he must stop doing the most normal thing in the world, namely treating his own perception as something that serves a purpose. This is the attitude a perceiving person has to his perception when he—to say it colloquially—isn't doing anything about it: The attitude that comes about on its own. Perception is, at least as a rule, a functioning instrument with which the perceiver pursues his own interests in the world. It serves successful action and is more successful the less attention is paid to its operation. A person using his perception to pursue a goal is intentionally with the matter at hand, but not with his perception. And this transparency of perception is exactly what changes when someone takes an artificial attitude with respect to perception. A person's perception is brought into an artificial state of operational orientation when the perceiver has no interest in the existence of what is being perceived. As mentioned earlier, disinterestedness and indifference as crucial conditions of possibility for an aesthetic judgment of taste were described as early as Kant in the *Critique of Judgment*: "One must not be in the least prepossessed in favor of the existence of the thing, but must preserve complete indifference in this respect, in order to play the part of judge in matters of taste."[2]

One example would be a sports car: This would be an object of aesthetic perception only if the observer were completely indifferent as to whether the car runs or has broken down, and especially if the observer does not have the slightest interest in owning or driving it. When he "makes abstraction"[3] from any purpose the thing might serve, the observer sees it as if it were a sculpture. The presentation of the car on a pedestal in a museum would facilitate this "simply *contemplative*"[4] way of looking. The object is then shown in such a decontextualized and detached way that it would be immediately clear to anyone that the concern is not about use, but solely about the way the thing is perceived. That becomes especially clear if—with absolutely no concern with its purpose—the car is hung on the wall like a picture.

But apart from whether it is through the attitude of the observer or the form of presentation, perception loses its usual instrumental character through indifference with regard to purpose and through disinterest in

A special aesthetic experience **89**

whether the thing exists or not. So, perception is implemented for its own sake. The observer continues to look at aesthetic things only because he would like to remain in the mental state of looking at the things. If this is the case, then we are dealing with that operationally oriented perception "for which," as Seel aptly writes, "the act of perception itself becomes the primary purpose of perception. One can also speak of a perception that is an end in itself. When such perception is operating, what is at issue is the way this perception operates" (tr.).[5]

## Features of aesthetic experience II: self-referentiality

If an operational orientation toward perception is a necessary feature of any aesthetic perception, the *second* feature, self-referentiality, is the sufficient one, for the perceiver certainly does not get aesthetic experiences from every perception for the sake of perception. The phenomenon of aesthetic perception is realized only if an operationally oriented perception is transformed into a self-referential experience.

This self-referentiality consists in the perceiver becoming aware, through the perception, that he himself is a perceiver. It amounts to an experience in which the one experiencing himself becomes the content of the experience. In this kind of self-referentiality, which is inherent in aesthetic experience, we are not dealing with a simple, conscious self-reflection, in which a perceiver is willfully paying attention to what it is like to be a perceiver. Seel describes this too:

> When I just said that in aesthetic perception we are present to ourselves as bodily-sensually perceiving beings, I did not mean that one's own perceptual activity was the actual object of this perception. That would be completely misleading. Aesthetic perception is not in general a perception of perception. [...] Aesthetic perception does not necessarily reflect on its own operation or on its own conditions (tr.).[6]

We can further say, that in an aesthetic perception the perceiver notices or feels himself to be a perceiver; he becomes present to himself as a perceiver. It concerns an effect of presence, a form of the perceiver's self-apprehension as to what he is: A perceiving human being.

**90** The Dadaism of possession

It amounts to a sensing of actual human presence—and that is "not only as a being who is aware of herself, but rather as a being deliberately letting her bodily sensorium perform" (tr.).[7]

There is no question that this idea of an inherent self-referentiality also originates in Kant's *Critique of Judgment*. Although Kant did not use the expression *aesthetic experience*, he uses the example of beauty to describe self-referentiality as the key feature of such a special experience. On the whole, his way of describing beauty is a model for an understanding of luxury, since the similarity of the two themes is clear. In much the same way the investigation of luxury developed, Kant, too, recognizes that the beauty of something is not a measurable feature of the thing—unless we are using the concept "feature" in the sense of a *disposition*, that beauty "lends itself to"[8] transporting people into an exceptional state of mind. The judgment *the rose is beautiful* is as much a grammatical illusion as the judgment *the chocolates are a luxury*. Kant declares the beauty of something solely from the setting in which a disinterested observer finds himself face-to-face with the beautiful. This setting consists, in the case of beauty, of "the state of mind involved in the free play of imagination and understanding."[9] But that basically means that for Kant, the word beautiful is nothing other than an everyday word to describe a state or setting phenomenologically, really the way someone feels about something. And this feeling is marked not only by pleasure or displeasure, but rather again by a particular content that justifies speaking of the state of experiencing beauty as an anthropologically pregnant moment, as a moment that is "attended with a feeling of the furtherance of life."[10] That is, in fact, Kant's main thesis, which he presents right away in the first paragraphs of the *Critique of Judgment*: The beautiful produces a "feeling of life" [*Lebensgefühl*].[11] To put it another way: In aesthetic experience, the living subject is referred to his perceptual capacities and, so, to himself. For Kant, the aesthetic experience is "a feeling which the subject has of itself."[12] In short, for Kant, the experience of beauty is a special experience—an anthropologically pregnant moment.

## Luxury: a special aesthetic experience

In claiming that luxury is a special form of aesthetic experience, what needs to be demonstrated is that *not only* luxury is based on a special experience. For every aesthetic experience is already a special experience

A special aesthetic experience **91**

*per se*, namely an operationally oriented and self-reflexive one. It must also be shown that among various aesthetic experiences, luxury once again presents an exception. If it didn't sound so peculiar, we could say that a phenomenology of luxury describes a *special special experience*—once more, in the case of luxury, the special, operationally oriented and self-reflexive experience comes about in a special way. What is special about the way it happens can be easily indicated: Aesthetic experience of luxury comes about through the act of possession. In fact we can anticipate—even before showing that luxury actually is an aesthetic experience at all—what its special qualities are with respect to other aesthetic experiences.

Thinking of aesthetic experience exclusively as a *special perceptual experience* unnecessarily narrows and reduces the broad spectrum of possible forms of aesthetic experience. But as a rule, that is exactly the case in reception aesthetics, and so the apparently obvious basic assumption states: A person has an aesthetic experience when his own perception is changed. But the concept of experience—like that of familiarity—is clearly broader than that of sense perception. Every perception of something is in fact always also an experience of this something, yet experience and familiarity are by no means fully realized in perception. If someone has experience with something, that experience is based on multiple forms of entering-into-a-relation-to-this-something. Even if it is not always the case, experiences are sometimes real encounters with something—an actual, multiply enmeshed kind of relationship between a person and the world, which is based, *only among other things*, on the sense perception of an object. Through actions, through the use of something, through experiments with something, through engagements—through conflict as through love—experiences are made, in broad terms, in and with the world through narratives. Experiences have a complexity that exceeds simple sense perception. Memories, expectations fulfilled and failed, emotional impressions as well as reflections, judgments, evaluations, interests and skills are involved in experiences—and aesthetic matters engage this complexity in its full scope. Such things need not be approached exclusively in an indifferent, disinterested way, but rather may be experienced in multiple ways. This is not to say that an aesthetic experience can come about without any sense perception of this thing at all. Sense perception is

**92 The Dadaism of possession**

presumed for any kind of experience. But even in reading a novel we have aesthetic experiences that we can hardly continue to understand as modifications of a sense perception given at the moment of reading. For what is perceived with the eyes is, at the moment of reading, just the book in the reader's hands. So the concept of aesthetic experience, unlike the concept of aesthetic perception, includes the reception of a text.

When we turn to the experience of luxury, it becomes important that the concept of aesthetic experience takes in much more than that of aesthetic perception. For here, we are concerned with that special case of aesthetic experience which is in fact based on a sense perception, namely of the luxury good—there is no doubt about that—but for which perception alone is not enough to provide an aesthetic experience of luxury. That was meant to be clear from the example of the personnel in the luxury hotel, who see, hear, touch and smell the same hotel as the guests. If the beauty of something rests exclusively on sense reception by way of smelling, hearing, touching and seeing, we can certainly say that the hotel personnel, too, can have the aesthetic experience of the hotel's beauty—but not of its luxury. The critical difference is that the personnel, in their situation, cannot experience the utterly excessive objects as luxury. This is because the reception of luxury is achieved through experiences based on a simultaneous *perception of and control over something*.

At least, this is the idea that gives luxury its special position among aesthetic phenomena. The usual recipient of an aesthetic object in the many theories of aesthetic experience is someone who is seeing, hearing or even perhaps reading—but not ordinarily one who is possessing. Seel lists exactly the modes of experience to which philosophical aesthetics ordinarily ascribes the possibility of being transformed in an aesthetic experience:

> In aesthetic perception we don't simply see, hear, feel, smell, taste and imagine something, we perform our seeing as seeing, our hearing as hearing, our touch as touch, our smelling as smelling, our tasting as tasting, our feeling as feeling, our imagining as imagining, our understanding as understanding (tr.).[13]

And—the critical extension and invention goes—*our possessing as possessing*. It seems that until now aesthetics and philosophy have simply

A special aesthetic experience **93**

and completely overlooked the possibility that for the possessor, the possession of things could, like other experiences, provide an experience of aesthetic transformation. Until now, possession has not been considered a possible form of reception for aesthetic experiences. But that is exactly the thesis: Luxuries are things of the world that let possession be experienced as possession. They resist the intentional transparency of possession, that is, the kind of possession in which the act of possession has no actuality, no presence for the possessor. Luxury goods, this much can now be claimed, do not constitute a group of things with particular ontological features. Rather their existence depends on a mode of opaque possession available in principle to subjects. Not only the viewer, but also the possessor of something, has experiences of this thing. Possession is an intentional relationship: The possessor has a consciousness of the object as a possessed object. So the thesis of the special aesthetic experience of luxury says that we can speak of luxury when and only when the possessor of something experiences a modification in his intentional experience of possession —and in fact not just any kind of modification, but exactly that kind in which possession as possession is experienced first in operational orientation and, second, with reference to himself. This is only possible, however, because the *possession of something*—in contrast to *ownership*—always requires the possessor to be aware of his possession.

## Ownership *versus* possession

For once, two concepts that can be defined, at least philosophically, largely without difficulties: Ownership and *possession*. The usual lexical distinctions and definitions are sufficient: Something is possessed if that thing is at some person's disposal. "The possession of something," as §854 of the *Civil Law Code* has it, "is attained through the acquisition of actual power over the thing." The critical point about this is that the possessor actually exercises physical dominance. It does not matter how the person came to have control or to dominate something. Even a thief is a possessor, at least if, after the theft, he has the object in his power, has control of it and intends to hold on to it for the sake of possession: *Animus rem sibi habendi*. However—and luckily—because of its illegal acquisition, the object has not become the thief's property. Under the term *ownership* we do not understand

**94** The Dadaism of possession

an actual, practical domination of something as we do under the term *possession*, but rather exclusively the *abstract right* to have control over something. If someone owns something, that person has a legally protected and assured possibility of control—quite apart from whether he makes use of this possibility or not.

The difference between an owner and a possessor is particularly important for the description of luxury because the aesthetic experience of luxury is bound up with the possession of something, but not with the issue of property—and by no means everyone who owns property also possesses it. Only the possessor actually uses, applies and employs the thing, and this performance of possession shows that he has an interest in the object—very much in Kant's sense—which is not always the case for property owners. The existence of the object is therefore not a matter of indifference to him. Possession ends in a different way: "The possession of an object is ended at the point the possessor abandons or in some other way loses actual power over the thing" (§856 *Civil Law Code*). That does not mean that a possessor of things possesses them only in those specific, often short, moments when he is actually using them, although the use of something is certainly the way in which the possession of something is most clearly enacted. Still, it is possible to possess things without being immediately aware of them or using them. "An interruption in the exercise of power, temporary by its nature, does not bring possession to an end" (§856 *Civil Law Code*). In juristic texts, the dominance of the possessor is therefore appropriately designated as a *relationship of proximity* of the possessor to what is possessed, which does not mean that he is physically close to the thing, but that he is closely involved with it. One can therefore have a relationship of proximity to something even if the thing is distant in a spatial sense; for example to a holiday flat far away that needs continual attention at home. Even if the flat itself is hardly ever used, one who shows his interest in the existence of the flat through his care is still a possessor. Conversely, if someone is unconcerned about the deterioration, misuse or destruction of his property, it suggests that in this case he is merely its owner, but not its possessor. For the possession of something demands an active possessor making decisions about the thing.

With respect to the difference between *property-holding* and *possession*, it is not surprising that in German there is a verb form, *possess* [*besitzen*] for the substantive form *possession* [*Besitz*]. Possession is an actual

A special aesthetic experience **95**

domination or use by a person; it requires an active person. Possessing is an activity, namely nothing less than the exercise of a will in relation to something, in the end always some way of using the thing. In contrast to this, it is for good reason that German has no corresponding verb for the substantive *property* [*Eigentum*]. It can be neither said nor thought that *someone properties something*. The owning of property is not an activity. For this reason it is possible to own property and not know anything about it. That does not happen to a possessor. Someone really in control of something, who is taking some trouble over it or using it himself, knows what he is doing. This must be the case for the concept to make sense: Any possession assumes the existence of a subject who knows that he possesses it, behaves in such a way as to maintain his possession, and also unquestionably has the phenomenal experience of what it is like to be the one who possesses this thing. Possessors of things can report what it is like to be their possessors—and many have tales to tell. Anyone who does not want to know what it is like to be a possessor cannot possess anything—experiences with possession are otherwise unavoidable.

We are dealing with a proper correlation *a priori*: Just as a possessor has to know that he possesses something in order to be a possessor, so a possession is always a possession for someone. For this simple, but crucial, reason, only the possession of something—by contrast to the ownership of property—lends itself to phenomenological consideration and, in the case of the possession of luxury, attracts phenomenological interest. So the thesis of what follows will be: Luxurious things are things that are what they are because they are possessed in a particular way. The luxurious is related to possession as the beautiful is to perception. A possessor who possesses a luxury performs possession first as operationally oriented possession, and second self-reflexively, so as to have an experience of himself. But the trick is: The description of luxury already actually showed that this was the way things stood. In Kantian style, we could say that we could draw the consequences of this explanation of luxury from the explanation just given, as *any effort that exceeds both what is technically necessary for something and what is anthropologically necessary for someone.*

## Luxury: operationally oriented possession

It is almost too simple, the situation is completely analogous. Just like the perception of something, the possession of something can be realized in an

**96** The Dadaism of possession

operationally oriented way, and is apparently realized in this way in more than a few cases, namely whenever someone possesses something for the sake of possession. For an example of the phenomenon of someone buying something simply because he wants to have it, we do not necessarily have to think of classic collectors. There are multiple reasons the condition of being a possessor can become the reason for possessing—and one gets the impression that the number of possible reasons is increasing. Wolfgang Ullrich, in the book mentioned in Chapter 3, *Habenwollen* [Wanting to Have], has made an impressive start on showing the range of these possible reasons. There is more than simple joy or pleasure in possessing. People can be proud of possession, which at least demonstrates that there are phenomenal ways of being a possessor. The most important motive for wanting to have something in a modern society is "the development of the way the thing functions as a portrait" (tr.).[14] But whatever reason a person may single out from the state of being a possessor as the real reason for possessing, the principle idea goes: Possessing something is, for the possessor, bound up with qualia, and these qualia can become the reason for possessing. Through the act of possessing, the possessor's purpose is then fulfilled. Something is bought or stolen in order to become its possessor; something inherited or received is kept for the same reason. From this standpoint, Erich Fromm's famous alternative *To Have or to Be* is not a complete disjunction. And it must be said, as is often the case, hybrid or ambivalent phenomena are exciting. The *having of something* may be sought for the sake of *being-as-one-who-has*. The most radical form of this possession for the sake of possession is attained when all symbolic functions of the self-presentation through possession are declared to be irrelevant, for symbolic functions too are still functions. We can speak of a "pure" self-reflexive function when the act of possessing and the emergence of a will to possess dominate the purpose of the activity to such an extent that the resulting experience of possession is the only thing that remains at issue. Only then are we dealing with operationally oriented, self-referential possession. The actions that secure and maintain possession then serve to perform this possession as such. It remains to say: The possession is not looked after and maintained in order to preserve the thing; that is rather done so as to maintain the mental state of possession. To push it a little further: In performing possession for possession's sake, the possessor is caring for himself, because the sense and purpose of the operationally oriented possession is the "feeling of possession" brought about by possession—to use a concept of Erich Fromm's.[15]

There is a common ground that permits the perception and the possession of something to be realized with the same operationally orientated performance. But this should not be allowed to deflect us from the understanding that this does not happen in the same way. The difference is easy to describe if we once again reach back to Kant's concept of disinterestedness. For Kant, disinterestedness is a necessary condition for modifying perception so that it becomes operationally oriented perception; the perceiver must remain indifferent with respect to the existence of the object, otherwise it is impossible to perceive it for perception's sake.

Here the parallel ends: When we apply Kant's concept of interest to the phenomenon of *possession for possession's* sake, it is immediately clear that there is such a thing as a disinterested perception, but no such thing as disinterested possession. For Kant, there is a correlation that can be clearly formulated between a person's interest on the one hand, and the existence of something on the other, namely that "although we have no interest whatever in the object, i.e. its real existence may be a matter of indifference to us."[16] Conversely, for Kant, whoever possesses something has, *a priori*, an interest in the existence of the object, for the possessor of something is just the one who is not indifferent. If he were indifferent, he would not be a possessor, but at the very most an owner.

Conceptual analysis reveals these dependencies: The state of possessing is defined by someone who finds himself in this state, really being interested in the thing. The state of possessing implies a *being-interested-in-possessing*. Someone with no interest in a thing therefore cannot, for Kant, be its possessor. In short: The idea of disinterested possession is a contradiction in itself. However, this is not to say that the situation with operationally oriented possession couldn't present itself somewhat differently.

There is no doubt, even in operationally oriented possession, an interest in the existence of the thing is given. We should not refute it, but neither should we fail to notice that interest in the existence of something is different for the operationally oriented possessor: It is not inhibited, but is made relative. That is, this interest is not artificially reduced to indifference in operationally oriented possession as it is in operationally oriented perception. In a state of operational orientation it is rather made relative through an additional interest: Someone who

**98** The Dadaism of possession

possess a luxurious cashmere sweater for the sake of possessing it not only has an interest in the sweater's existence, but also an interest in implementing possession. And exactly because this further interest in implementation is present, it can no longer be said that this act of possession is solely concerned with an interest in the thing. Interest in the existence of the thing is not contemplatively reduced to indifference, then, but rather de-monopolized, in some sense, through an additional interest. When something is possessed for the sake of possession, then the inherent interest in the existence of the thing—necessary for the act of possession—is fully realized once again, for reasons that have nothing to do with the existence of something as a means to an end. One is interested in the possession of the thing even more than in the thing itself. The fulfillment of a desire to possess no longer takes precedence, not because of an interest in the thing for some purpose, but because this interest in something has been overshadowed by a real interest in the state of possession. This certainly does not justify speaking of a disinterested possession, but of a possession in which the existence of the thing is no longer the predominant reason for possessing.

The description of operationally oriented possession need not remain abstract. On the contrary, there is an indicator that can be used—to some extent by outsiders—to confirm when someone has a possession for possession's sake. This indicator involves an evaluation that the possessor gives about the maintenance of his possession, for it may be uncontroversial. If a thing is possessed in a goal-oriented way—as a means to an end—then all efforts to care for it, to keep it in good condition or even just functional are nothing more than other means, namely means to the end of keeping the means functional. From the perspective of a goal-oriented possessor, the necessity of protecting and caring for an instrumental possession appears as an undesirable side effect, occasionally even as something bad that cannot be avoided if the instrument is to be of service. As a result, this possessor will always find things that require less protection and care, that are more and more efficient, to be more practical, for the goal-oriented possessor is interested in the thing's function, not in its maintenance.

The situation is completely different if someone possesses something for the purpose of possession itself rather than in a goal-oriented way.

A special aesthetic experience **99**

Then the obligation to maintain it inevitably becomes a supplemental reason for possessing the thing. The possessor's attitude and approach to the care of the possession changes fundamentally in this situation. It may be unnecessary to ask what is conditioning what in this case: Whether the operational orientation changes the possessor's attitude to maintenance or, conversely, the possessor's changed attitude produces an operationally oriented possession. Either way, the attitude toward maintenance for goal-oriented possession is completely different from that for operationally oriented possession.

A few examples. If a garden is possessed for the sake of possession, it will not be possessed exclusively for a purpose—say, for therapy—but at least as much for the opportunity to plan and care for it. A house possessed for the sake of possession also fulfills the purpose of providing the inhabitant with the possibility of remodelling and furnishing it. We are dealing with a principle: In the case of something possessed because one wants to possess it, the effort and the means that enable a possession to serve its purpose must themselves become the purpose of possessing. This means that if a complex, elaborate automobile is to become the object of a luxury experience, it must have a possessor who treats it as not only a means of transport, but who also has it in order to be able to repair, scrutinize and clean it. A bill for fuel or repairs does not appear to such a possessor as a bad, regrettably unavoidable thing he must put up with so as to be able to drive the car, but rather as a kind of investment in something authentic—which, however, does not make it more pleasant or even easier to pay. Conversely, we can conclude that someone who possesses an automobile—even one that is far too elaborate and madly complicated—without the additional purpose of protecting and caring for it, is not possessing it in an operationally oriented way and so does not fulfill the necessary condition for the kind of possession that can become an experience of luxury. For the aesthetic experience of luxury is bound up with an operationally oriented possession, and this kind of possession goes in turn with a specific attitude toward maintenance. For this reason, someone's record collection can only be experienced as a luxury when this collection is no longer compiled exclusively for listening to music, but rather when the compilation itself, the constant resorting and reordering themselves become an equally important reason. Think of the record enthusiast Rob in Nick

**100** The Dadaism of possession

Hornby's novel *High Fidelity*. The instrumental reason—one has the collection in order to listen to music—is here made relative as one reason among others of equal value.

In principle, this interaction with one's own relationship to one's own possession is possible with any possession. Anything that can be a possession can be possessed for the sake of possession. But if, in the performance of this act of possession for possession's sake, the possessor experiences a feeling of life—as Kant would say—a palpable presence of his own human existence as a free being, exactly then and only then does this thing present us with an instance of luxury.

## Luxury's self-referentiality

The operationally oriented possession of luxury goods is defined by the self-referentiality of the experience of possession for the possessor—and this for an extremely simple reason. This reason concerns the conditions of possibility for luxury: A possessor of luxury goods must take the view that his possession is superfluous and inappropriately exaggerated for human beings. Otherwise, he could not and would not believe he possessed a luxury good. The interpretation of something as not necessary is in turn necessary—and not only that. It is equally necessary for the interpreter to hold this interpretation to be true. This is not to say that it is true! Since luxury is bound up with the interpreter's phenomenal experience, it finally depends on his inner perspective: On holding-to-be-true and not on being-true. This personal holding-to-be true necessarily produces—if the interpreter and the possessor are identical—the experience of surpassing, by means of the possession, his own conviction about what is usual and proper. That is: Through his possession, a person enters into a self-reflexive relationship with his own self-understanding—and does so by surpassing it.

In intentionally transgressing a boundary, the one crossing the boundary becomes aware of the boundary. In the case of luxury, that can only mean that an understanding of human beings becomes appreciable through relationships of possession; it amounts to becoming palpably aware of having overcome, through one's own possession, an inner resistance. In order for this to happen, it is not enough for the object to be linguistically interpreted and described as luxury; that can just as well be done by an outsider who does not himself possess the

A special aesthetic experience **101**

object in question. No one behaves improperly or inappropriately just by examining or speaking about luxury. The aesthetic experience of luxury is bound up with one's own possession of luxury because the state of possession is binding on the subject. That is to say: A person who just observes something that crosses the boundary of what is appropriate has not, through such an act of reception through examination, himself crossed the boundary. Now the viewer may in fact also be responsible for what he is examining—still, by seeing, hearing, reading, smelling and touching alone, there is no *existence-defining phenomenal repercussion* for the subject. To put it another way: Someone who listens to a Dadaist poem does not himself become a Dadaist; the subject does not himself become what the thing is. The situation is completely different if this thing has been bought, stolen, used and possessed. For unlike a reader, who assumes no responsibility for the content of a novel, the possessor takes full responsibility for his possession. This certainly does not apply to all features of the possession, but it does to those relevant to its status as luxury. Someone who possesses things with extravagant, irrational characteristics becomes an extravagant, irrational person himself, and this with the desired effect of therefore also knowing, as such a possessing person, what it is like to be autonomous with respect to the demands of instrumental rationality. Someone who only sees the extravagant or reads about it does not know this effect. We are rather concerned with an existential self-referentiality of the subject, typical of aesthetic experiences, made possible in this case through the intentional act of possession. Surprisingly, this is confirmed in particular by Walter Benjamin.

It may come as a complete surprise that no other philosopher matches Walter Benjamin in celebrating the phenomenal quality of a relationship to the world made possible through private possession, in all its aesthetic particularity. In the end, Benjamin left no doubt of his sympathies with a communist form of society. But considering that Benjamin repeatedly developed theses in his aesthetic writings that deliberately contradict the aesthetic ideals of the educated classes, the description of possession in his short, autobiographical essay, "Unpacking My Library" of 1931, is perhaps not so remarkable. Benjamin appears to be deliberately seeking out the places where one can have aesthetic experiences that do not meet middle-class expectations. Even the most famous essay, "The Work of Art in the Age of

**102** The Dadaism of possession

its Mechanical Reproducibility," defends cinema in this sense, as a place of aesthetic experience *sui generis* that does not conform to the middle-class ideal that an aura must be perceived in the reception of art. In a parallel way, in "Unpacking My Library" he describes possession as an act of aesthetic experience that is not consistent with the middle-class ideal of disinterested perception either. Almost mockingly, he demonstrates this aesthetic experience gained through possession using the example of the very object that is most highly valued in the world of the educated classes: The book. Benjamin, too, holds his books in the highest esteem—but not on account of their content. He is concerned to describe the book as an example of a "relationship ... to possessions"[17] that is possible in principle: "a relationship to objects which does not emphasize their functional, utilitarian value."[18] Benjamin's thesis could hardly have been more testing for intellectuals. In reduced form, it states: The buying and owning of books opens on to more interesting aesthetic experience than does the reading of books. Benjamin expressly values the "thrill of acquisition"[19] more highly than the comparatively bland aesthetic experiences that may be brought about by reading books. Benjamin's description corresponds to the difference already indicated between reading and seeing on the one hand and owning and having on the other. The phenomenal repercussion, that by owning it, the possessor himself partially becomes what the possession is, corresponds to Benjamin's idea that possession "is the most intimate relationship that one can have to objects."[20] Wolfgang Ullrich's commentary on this quotation is particularly apt: "The desire to have and the joy of having seem to evoke feelings that are more existential than an engagement with contents" (tr.).[21]

## Intellectuals' resentment of an aesthetic of possession

From a certain perspective it seems simply incomprehensible that intellectuals' aesthetic perspectives could not be smoothly integrated with the idea that luxury arises from a special form of aesthetic experience, for there actually appears to be a basic common ground between luxury and education. The educated classes—whatever we take that to mean—in any case defend a form of life in which instrumental rationality in certain questions is actually distained. The striving for

A special aesthetic experience **103**

education—that is, the intellectual ideal—is always a striving toward a comprehensive, wide-ranging and profound knowledge that is much more than just a means adapted to reaching desirable goals. Even Adorno, one of the harshest critics of the intellectual classes, has to recognize that the cultivation of education undermines instrumental rationality. In his *Theorie der Halbbildung* [Theory of Half Education] of 1959, Adorno explicitly states that "Freedom from the diktat of means, of stolid and meager usefulness" is the "dream of education" (tr.).[22] However, Adorno was also of the opinion, for whatever reasons, that the dream could not be realized, in any case not through education. But apart from that, for the relationship between education and luxury it is first essential that both friends of luxury and friends of education defend the view that a successful life is achieved not solely in pursuit of what is pleasant, practical and purposeful. Seen in this way there is a kind of shared fate. In a society dominated by instrumental and utilitarian thinking, education and luxury seem equally unnecessary, as too much unnecessary knowledge in the one case, and too much unnecessary effort in the other. This basic common ground in terms of attitude makes it seem incomprehensible at first glance that there would be or should be a firm intellectual critique of luxury.

The critique is of a different kind. The intellectual way of seeing—when it is constructed in idealized form—makes a clear distinction between critics of luxury that stand in the tradition of Jean-Jacques Rousseau or of Thorstein Veblen. It is not a moral critique of the way luxury phenomena always involve unnecessary effort. In fact it cannot be that, for such a technocratic critique of a refusal of utilitarian thinking would apply equally to its own high esteem for education. The intellectual critique of luxury—and this is why it is to be taken seriously—is rather a decidedly aesthetic critique, typically advanced by self-proclaimed lovers of art and friends of beautiful things. They defend without limitation the view that the visiting of art museums and theatres, the reading of novels and listening to classical music is an irreplaceable form of human self-awareness and enlightenment—that is, of education.

But—and this form of critique begins exactly with this *but*—the principal assessment of the aesthetic from the standpoint of the educated classes is bound up with the view that the noble ambitions of a cultural life of the mind—the *recognition of the true*, the *doing of good*,

**104** The Dadaism of possession

the *perception of the beautiful*—have nothing to do with possession. The very idea that there could be a kind of play with aesthetic experience for which possession of an aesthetic object would be an important condition seems like something impermissible. Educated people are deeply convinced that human beings can have all relevant forms of aesthetic experience without having to possess anything to do so. Luxury cannot be aesthetically relevant because a world in which something culturally and anthropologically relevant was associated with possession would be a bad world. This is not to cast doubt on whether luxury goods can have aesthetic dimensions. However, the aesthetic aspects of luxury goods are considered to be only those sensual attractions stimulated by aesthetic things, or aesthetic things used as status symbols to show off. Because they do not contribute to the experience of self and the education of a person, they are considered in every case to be aesthetically trivial phenomena. This view is actually celebrated as an enlightened achievement, if not actually as emancipation. The early phenomenologist Moritz Geiger, today effectively forgotten, characterized this spirit with reference to Kantian aesthetic as follows: "The democracy of experience runs in its blood; it wants to level things out" (tr.).[23] And he is right. In raising disinterest, indifference and unconcern with possession to the level of the condition of possibility for aesthetic experience, Kant at the same time made this experience available to anyone, in a sense democratized it. We are dealing with one—perhaps the most important—ideal of the educated classes, which is rightly represented as such in the literature. Here Wolfgang Ullrich is especially on target:

> Everything beautiful was rather interpreted as a public good and treated using the model of beauty in nature: just as anyone has the opportunity to see a landscape, a field with flowers or a sunset, and just as no one needs to concern himself with questions of property while doing so, so should it be with art. Museums came into being in the trail of this understanding, where, in the collections, a person could find, as Novalis formulated it, "a lover and a friend, a fatherland and a god", but where a desire to possess was ruled out from the start (tr.).[24]

A special aesthetic experience **105**

Now the question is not whether Kant was right, that the experience of beauty and of art is bound up with disinterest. This can be agreed. Rather the question is whether it is right to believe, in his sense, that *all* aesthetic experiences are necessarily bound to the recipient's attitude of disinterest. The concern is with the claim to exclusivity. What speaks against a plurality of phenomena? More exactly: What speaks against there being aesthetic experience without and with an interest in possession, such as the aesthetic experience of beauty and of luxury? The effect of the Kantian aesthetic on the educated classes led to the widespread view that aesthetic experience in all its forms, without exception, occurs only when no interest in the existence of the thing is given. But that also means that any kind of question about who owns the object is simply unimportant for the description of aesthetic phenomena. And the critical point is that this way of seeing could actually be endorsed without restriction—if we were speaking only of property rather than of possession.

In its view of luxury, the intellectual position does not distinguish between *possession as actual control over something* and *ownership as an abstract right to control something*. For the latter, the skeptical and hostile position is completely persuasive. Legal property relationships as well as the recipient's financial options are perfectly irrelevant to any form of aesthetic experience of the objects in question; they simply play no part. Yet, if we handle the actual act of possessing something in this way, as if the legal property relationships were what was meant, we would be working with a crude reduction. For, as already described, the possession of something, in contrast to ownership—is a mental state with intentionality: possession is always a conscious possession of something, and so a human relationship to the world or to the thing. It, like all relationships to the world, permits an aesthetic transformation and offers the possibility of an aesthetic experience. If this were not the case, the mental act of possessing something would have to be considered an exception among intentional states. Possession would then have a very odd and inexplicable special position. For people can engage in hearing things, seeing things, depicting things, smelling things, touching things, moving things, telling things, designing things, building things, making things, eating things, imagining things, dealing with things in an operationally-oriented way that transmits a self-referential *feeling of life* to them in the form of an aesthetic

**106** The Dadaism of possession

experience. The possessing of things would stand out all alone in a great empire of many intentional states, since it is not accepted as a mental and intentional experience that also sustains aesthetic experience—because what may not be cannot be, namely that a culturally or aesthetically germane phenomenon of possession, misunderstood as ownership, is relevant.

Against this background, the fact that luxury has so far played no role as a form of aesthetic experience *sui generis* in any of many philosophical theories of aesthetic experience becomes, or may become, an *expression phenomenon* [*Ausdrucksphänomen*]. For there may be many reasons why philosophy seems so far to have had no interest in an aesthetic of possession. One explanation would be that to overlook or ignore it is an affirmative expression of an implicit pattern of liberal intellectual thinking, which shapes academic aesthetics at least as tenaciously as it does middle-class museum culture.

We could go a step further and ask what the reason actually is for middle-class stigmatization of ownership and possession as a form of aesthetic reception. How did it come to this intractable attitude? Wolfgang Ullrich offers a suggestion that is historical, or more precisely, art historical. In his essay "Besitzen statt rezipieren" [Possession Instead of Receiving] of 2014 he refers to historical property relationships of works of art to explain the middle-class rejection of the view that one could have genuine aesthetic experience in the act of possession: "We are concerned here with a typical case of hypercompensation: In coming to terms with a deficit, a new norm arose which largely negated that against which one had wanted to assert oneself" (tr.).[25] The reference is to the following correlation:

> In the eighteenth century, citizens were at most onlookers with respect to art; it happened almost exclusively in the circles of the nobility and the wealthy, who functioned — roles being distributed differently in individual cases — as commissioners, buyers and patrons [...] Only sluggishly, incompletely and after repeated demands from representatives of the middle class were the art collections of the courts and nobility made public in the late eighteenth century [...] That also means, however, that it was not customary to look at art as an outsider, that is, to encounter it as its recipient. Someone who commissions it or

A special aesthetic experience **107**

owns it experiences it as a part of his daily life. He has no further need to demonstrate anything with respect to it [...] An onlooker, on the other hand, if he does not want to remain such an onlooker forever, uses his viewing of art to reach clever judgments, gain knowledge, show himself to be especially well informed or subtle. [...] The energetic interaction with art in modern times really did grow out of a sense of deficit. To interpret works, to experience them consciously, to show oneself to be taken by them, even to reflect on them and to write, represents the educated classes' compensation for insufficient rights of access to art (tr.).[26]

## Luxury: a defiant Lebensgefühl

A thing can be luxury only if its possessor experiences it, through an operationally-oriented expression of his own desire to possess, as *something that exceeds, in effort, both what is technically necessary for something and what is anthropologically necessary for someone*. The characteristic feature of a luxury experience consists in feeling that one's own conception of what is really significant and important is not absolute. The life world basis for this experience of luxury is therefore a position of refusal. In luxury, the possessor has a direct experience of his own views about people as relative; by means of possession, he realizes that his own opinion, which is correct and appropriate, is not absolute; by means of his possession, he laughs at himself. That is clearly not an empirical description that rests on psychological research on possessors of luxury, but rather a quality necessary for the experience of luxury. If this phenomenal quality is not given, it would no longer make sense to speak of luxury. But that also means that in the experience of luxury, there comes a point of actual internal split. It cannot be so strong as to produce pangs of conscience, however. Transgression through excess in the zone prior to a bad conscience—that is luxury. For someone who is experiencing luxury must have a standard for what is appropriate, but must also break with this standard, which he himself recognizes, in order to be able to attain luxury as the liberating antithesis. This is the reason luxury often has a provocative effect on outsiders. The unwritten laws of restraint, the ordinary regulations of taste, the desirable

**108** The Dadaism of possession

forms of modesty and the ruling commands of rationality are over-stepped by being surpassed, by being *too much*. This does not mean that in order to be a luxury something has to be owned for the sake of provocation. It is to say that what is perceptible as provocation from the outside, to self-righteous people and know-it-alls is, from a first person singular perspective, namely that of the possessor of luxury, exactly what constitutes the attraction of luxury, namely doing something that contradicts general expectations and etiquette so as to enter into a relationship of autonomy with respect to one's own idea of rationality. Luxury cannot therefore be fully accounted for as sheer provocation. If it could, there would be a purpose in apparently luxurious things after all, namely a purpose that can be achieved only by means of something exaggerated. But luxury's experience of autonomy expressly forbids the purposeful, efficient pursuit of a goal—whatever it may be. Just as real social provocation cannot therefore be an intentional goal of luxury, so is the possibility of provocation given with luxury nevertheless an inherent quality of the experience of something as luxury, for the possessor has to know that he has something provocative in order for it to become a luxury for him. This ties the experience of luxury to a successful balancing act, using something provocative without using it for the sake of provocation.

It may well be realistic to suppose that people's views will vary on the question of which things, which intentions, which actions in human life qualify as rational. There is a broad spectrum of the most varied answers, of which more than a few make claims to general validity, of which more than a few mutually contradict one another. But the extreme variation among people in their ideas of appropriateness, forms of life and rationality does not mean there are no general principles in the ways people deal with these divergent ideas. One such principle goes: Even if they believe they know what is necessary, reasonable and appropriate in one case or another, people can nevertheless make a different decision—and do so voluntarily! The possibility of doing so is the condition of possibility for any experience of luxury. For the possession of luxury is definable in two aspects: On the one hand it is action in spite of knowing better, but on the other hand it is not a form of *akrasia*, a weakness of the will. On the contrary, it is not rare for the possession of luxury goods—especially their acquisition—to be based on thorough reflection and deliberations. It

A special aesthetic experience **109**

may be even more applicable to a well-planned theft. In both cases the key issue is that one does not come into the possession of goods that permit an experience of luxury against one's will, as a result of, say, seduction, or of actions one later regrets. For the constitution of an experience of luxury demands that reason be refused with an action that is as carefully considered as it is defiant. This defiant, wayward or petulant moment, necessarily inherent to luxury, may also be described as a kind of residual infantile disobedience—at least according to Peter Sloterdijk in *Nicht gerettet* [Not Recovered] of 2001, when he points out: "All luxury starts with permission to be immature and to retain and live out an infantile past."[27] Still, however we characterize this moment that belongs to the experience of luxury, only a deliberately rebellious action can lay claim to being a free decision, and so one capable of evoking the desired emotional reaction in this contrary way, namely, the palpable presence of a truly human capacity, which is to say, a capacity that the possessor may assume is to be found in any human subject.

We still have the question at hand of how an experience of luxury can be understood as the experience of an anthropologically pregnant moment. For to make the claim, it must be shown that the capacity that leads to an experience of self by means of an operationally oriented possession really is a capacity that anthropologically distinguishes human beings as human. But remarkably this seems to be the very thing that was verified in the last description, namely that such an ability does make itself felt in the experience of luxury. For a human being is singled out as human not only in having a unique idea of what is rational in each case, but also in being able to go on to take a position with respect to it—which in turn can occur rationally or irrationally.[28]

The barbarians in Friedrich Schiller's *On the Aesthetic Education of Man in a Series of Letters* (1795) are a good example of people who are *irrationally rational*, and therefore cannot, in Schiller's view, lead good, balanced lives. The person who is playing is, on the contrary, *rationally rational* for Schiller. In this context it makes no difference what form of life is considered to be rational by a particular person in a specific case. The one key point is: A person under any circumstances can only be called rational if he decides of his own free will in favor of that which from his standpoint seems to be rational, and that he does

**110** The Dadaism of possession

not do it slavishly, like a machine programmed for rationality. Being rational presumes that rationality is contingent. There is hardly any better example of this principle of human existence than the possession of luxury. Luxury does not, after all, resist an expectation that qualifies as reasonable and appropriate simply by ignoring this expectation in its justifiability. That would be the case if someone thought that only philistines consider a lavish five-course menu to be an unmitigated extravagance. Someone who finds luxury normal is not experiencing luxury. Someone who considers a dish that consists entirely of exotic delicacies to be an ordinary meal is not setting himself above a justifiable notion of appropriate effort, but rather is doubting the justification for this notion and thereby making it impossible to experience such a menu as luxury. Only someone who recognizes conventional norms is in a position to overstep them in the interests of experiencing autonomy. If this happens though operationally oriented possession, it leads to a specific phenomenal experience that can be called luxury. So it is right to say that luxury is when someone does something anyway, or in short: *Luxury is defiance.* Although it is certainly not the only one, this experience is not the least of those that show the human ability and need to voluntarily defy ideas recognized to be correct. Societies that build up pressure to be reasonable necessarily arrive at a dialectical situation: Someone who is forced, for whatever reasons, to do something reasonable will no longer act reasonably at all. For, as is the case with any action, part of acting reasonably is assuming responsibility for the action. In the same way a causally determined movement is not an action, a movement determined by reason would not be either. Whatever reasonable behavior might be, it requires a subject to perform these actions voluntarily in every case. One may welcome it or regret it, but it applies generally: A human being is a life-form that cannot be forced to be reasonable. Someone who is following reasonable rules purely out of fear of sanctions is, in fact, behaving in accordance with reason, but is not acting reasonably, because he is not deciding to act voluntarily and from conviction—and humans alone are credited with being able to do exactly that. It is a characteristic of human existence. Human beings can put themselves in a relationship to their own convictions and behave with this relation in mind. That takes many forms. Some people smoke voluntarily, although they are fully persuaded that it is

A special aesthetic experience **111**

absolutely unreasonable. Yet this disjunction hardly produces experiences of luxury, because it is a setting-oneself-beyond reasonable notions of health and not reasonable notions of effort. Only if, by possessing something irrational and improper, a person feels the characteristic thing about his existence—the ontological *existential* of eccentricity—does it make linguistic sense to call this possession a luxury.

With this, the basic idea is confirmed: Something becomes luxury in light of an experience of autonomy achieved through transgression in possession. Luxuries are very particular things, namely only those things whose possession allow a human being to feel, *qua* his own humanity, that he himself can once again reconsider his position to that which he himself takes to be reasonable. Among earthly beings, only humans have been endowed with this capacity for self-reflexive position-taking: For the constitution of a subject assumes a relationship to self. Unlike animals, people can reconsider necessities of nature, necessities of reason, established customs and practices, notions of appropriateness and reasonableness. Luxury arises not only, but not inconsequentially, from such an eccentric, position-related stance with respect to that which is considered useful, necessary and appropriate. For this reason luxury must necessarily have "the moment of liberation within it" (tr.)—as a pregnant insight of Georg Friedrich Wilhelm Hegel's goes in a transcript of his lecture *Philosophie des Rechts* [Philosophy of Right] of 1819–1820.[29] Here, the circle closes on the initial reflections on anthropologically relevant pregnant moments, for it is exactly this phenomenal quality of a liberation—a human freedom from the force of necessity felt in the experience of luxury—that enables us to think of luxury, too, as a functional equivalent. Luxury can also serve that function that Schiller attributed to play, to make it possible for a person to have a "complete intuition of his human nature."[30]

## The Dadaism of possession

Luxury, as a way of experiencing the presence of being, may, like so many things in the world, have different attractions for different people for different reasons. On the one hand, the statement is hardly a surprising one, and perhaps is almost banal, surely no one would

**112** The Dadaism of possession

claim for luxury what Schiller actually said about play, namely that there is one and only one way that a person *is entirely human only* [sic!] *when he is playing.* There are aesthetic alternatives that also produce a feeling of self. But, on the other hand, it is not surprising that luxury gains tremendous significance for societies at times when a hysterical drive for efficiency and accumulation predominates. Luxury necessarily becomes attractive against the background of a social situation. For, if we understand luxury to be an aesthetic experience of being as being, we can also say that luxury exists when someone manages, by means of owning something—whatever it looks like, however much or little it cost—to have the private experience of not succumbing to the rational function of machines. Put more succinctly, luxury is a Dadaism as we know it from art history: The revolt of nonconforming incivility against custom, propriety and especially against philistine notions of normalcy. But careful, this is not to defend as meaningful something that is not meaningful! We cannot say, that is, that the possession of something that demands a wasteful, exaggerated and superfluous effort is reasonable or meaningful. The concepts would no longer make sense. Not to use money, resources, work, materials, time and energy in appropriate, efficient and effective ways, that is, not to use them rationally, is unreasonable *per definitionem.* That cannot and will not be changed. This is the reason an experience of luxury is not a reasonable experience, but rather, a genuinely Dadaistic experience, whose quality Kurt Schwitters pinpointed wonderfully: "But there is sense in nonsense" (tr.).[31] Schwitters is, in fact, referring to his own art here, but his dictum applies unreservedly to luxury as well. In fact, we can well say that the transition from the extremely exaggerated demands of a luxury to a Dadaist happening can sometimes be fluid.

The effort of being uncivil, the break with philistine correctness preserves an experience of sense in its nonsense, namely that of not being dominated by reasonable views, obligations and morals. There are general principles of luxury that may be specified without having to say exactly what is reasonable. Are opera houses, saunas, grand pianos, bouquets of flowers, paperweights or horse riding unreasonable and extraneous expenditures of effort? A phenomenology of luxury has no need to enter into this discussion, for happily the key point lies beyond the specific question of who designates what to be reasonable

A special aesthetic experience **113**

or unreasonable: It is the intension rather than the extension of the concept of luxury that matters. This much can be said: The experience of luxury depends, with no if or buts, on the act of possession; without it a possessor has no such experience of nonconformist extravagance. But that does not mean, as one might incorrectly suppose, that the experience of luxury depends on the amount that is wasted, the size of the possession or even on wealth; grand possessions do not correspond to great experiences. The quality of an aesthetic experience of beauty does not correspond to the size of the beautiful object. It is possible to have an aesthetic experience with one of William Turner's small watercolors that is in no way inferior to the aesthetic experience of one of his large oil paintings; nor is one of Schwitters' great Dadaist assemblages any more Dadaistic that one of his small-format collages. Applied to luxury, this means that the experience of luxury is an experience of Dadaist freedom, available to its full extent with small as well as large possessions.

The structural affinity between the concepts *luxury* and *Dada* can be traced historically as well, at least they can definitely be found in the writings of the Swiss-Hungarian writer, artist and art collector Carl Laszlo. In 1967, Laszlo published some of his art manifestos under the programmatic title *Aufruf zum Luxus* [Call to Luxury]. Although he was trying in these texts to revive the attitudes and spirit of Dadaism from the beginning of the 20th century, he did not reach back to the concept of Dadaism to describe his own position. The reason for this is that from Laszlo's standpoint, the concept of Dadaism had lost its bearings through its use in the neo-Dada movement of the postwar period. In the manifesto "Bevor Neo-Dada da war, war Dada da" [Before Neo-Dada was there, there was Dada] of 1966, Laszlo distances himself from this movement that was, in his view, "geared exclusively to being noticed" (tr.).[32] This made it necessary, in Laszlo's view, to find a new concept that would express the original sense of Dada. His writings on this point offer one single great suggestion: The concept of luxury can take the place of Dada. The expressions *luxury* and *Dada* become synonyms in the title of the manifesto *Call to Luxury*—as, say, in a sentence such as: "Luxury lets us regard zealous missionaries and obtuse mass murderers with disgust" (tr.)[33] We can only understand such a sentence by assuming that Laszlo is using *luxury* and *Dada* with the same meaning.

**114** The Dadaism of possession

But the decisive methodological point is that the equating of luxury and Dada is not an idiosyncratic quirk unique to Laszlo. Rather, he recognizes a structural affinity or even an identity between the things. So, he says right away in the first sentence of his manifesto: "Luxury is freedom. Luxury can be attained by anyone, wealth cannot" (tr.).[34] We agree. It is easy to imagine life worlds and human situations in which a taxi journey or a polaroid photograph would be occasions for an experience of luxury—just because in many life contexts these things are hardly reasonable or efficient, but simply extravagant. Imagine a person who is, as a result of his poverty, dependent on charity for his livelihood. Yet this person does not—possibly to the benefactors' irritation—spend the small amounts he receives on urgent necessities and useful things. Instead, defying all reason, he boldly and insolently asserts his freedom to eat a piece of cream cake in the next café. That is Dadaism: Transgressing against what is useful and appropriate to the situation and, in the case of a Dadaism of luxury, by means of unreasonable effort. For this Dadaism, possession is necessary, but the decisive thing is the engagement of the one who wants to provoke an experience of the possessor's threatened ego. It works with small possessions; in fact one might even say it works better than it does with large ones. That surely does not apply as a matter of principle, but does suggest a dialectical phenomenon. For many a possessor of diverse villas, yachts and racehorses won't have such a Dadaistic experience of autonomy because they considers their property to be in keeping with their position–appropriate, suitable or even necessary—and do not consider the scale or complexity to be exaggerated at all. It is only the private awareness of one's ego bumping up against conventions by means of one's own possession, and even of doing something disproportionately extravagant and superficial that determines the specific quality of the aesthetic experience of luxury. It is not the size of the possession. This is the reason for the social hope, surely too broad and perhaps even utopian, that Carl Laszlo associated as much with luxury as with Dadaism: "Luxury makes us independent, courageous and honest" (tr.).[35]

This applies in a temporal respect as well. An experience of luxury can only last as long as the possession is felt by the possessor to resist a perceived normative expectation. We can describe a proportional dependence in reverse: Without the demand to be reasonable—however it may arise—there can be no experience of luxury, just as,

A special aesthetic experience **115**

conversely, with an increasingly widespread demand to be reasonable, luxury almost necessarily becomes an increasingly attractive *defiant aesthetic practice* of experiencing self and autonomy. It is this way of looking at luxury that correlates with the finding that in utilitarian life worlds infused with a sense of economic frugality in particular, the aesthetic experience of luxury exerts a strong attraction as an experience of liberation. In a similar way, a quiet longing for existentialism is felt in times of instrumental rationality gone wild. An existentialist does not know the aesthetic experience of luxury; he cannot know it. As Sartre's position made clear, he lacks any meaningful idea of what people actually need. And yet, it is worth noting that luxury makes people into part-time existentialists. Anyone who experiences luxury feels himself to be an existentialist in the brief moments of the experience, for in them he feels that he himself is condemned to freedom, that he must take a position even with respect to his own notions of rationality if they are to define him. With this specific phenomenal content of a luxury experience in view, the circle closes to Schiller's idea of an anthropologically pregnant moment. An experience of luxury is, in its phenomenal content, indistinguishable from the phenomenal content of the experience of play for Schiller: The concept of play for Schiller differs from the concept of luxury only intentionally, but not extensionally. It involves the same experience, the same mental state, the one or the other being addressed with two different words. These states cannot be distinguished by their phenomenal quality for the subject. But that means, as Schiller already said himself, only with another word: A human being feels luxury only when he is human in the full sense of the word, and *he is fully human when he is experiencing luxury*. But with respect to this sentence, even Schiller would have wanted to emphasize that what is meant by the formulation *experiencing luxury* is nothing like what is meant by *living in luxury*. For the question of whether a person is living in luxury can readily be answered by an outsider on good grounds. He can say why he thinks that certain things in a person's life are exaggerated, unreasonable and wasteful. But only the person in question knows whether he is experiencing luxury, just as only he himself knows whether he is playing, in a Schillerian sense. This is the reason luxury can be experienced without living in what is commonly understood to be luxury. And conversely, people can live in luxury without experiencing luxury.

**116** The Dadaism of possession

What is worrying is that in light of delusions of grandeur, greed and arrogance, or just naïveté and habit, this condition may not be at all uncommon. In short, to assert, with Schiller, that human beings are only human in the full sense of the word when they are living in luxury, is simply decadent and deceptive—just as decadent and deceptive as the view, as Schiller would say, that only people who are playing, as observed from the outside, so something like casino visitors, would be human in the full sense of the word. One does not reach a specific anthropologically pregnant moment in Schiller's tradition through a *life of luxury*, or through a *life of play*, either, but through an *experience of luxury* or *of play* respectively. We must be particularly attentive to this fine difference in taking up the criticism of luxury.

## What is open to criticism about luxury?

To describe luxury as an aesthetic experience is neither to praise nor to condemn it, and this for a simple reason. People cannot meaningfully be accused of experiencing a possession in a certain way—whether that be as emancipation or as conformity. People cannot really be praised for having particular experiences, either. Rather what applies to the experience of beauty also applies to the experience of luxury. What is morally noteworthy is not that there is such an aesthetic experience, it is rather exclusively what people do to try to have an experience of this kind. These actions—and buying, stealing and using are actions without a doubt—can and should, like all other actions, be morally evaluated, as difficult as this certainly is in many cases. The two principle possible results of such a moral evaluation are easy to define. It is easy to imagine and surely also to find humanly and socially detrimental actions that are justifiably criticized and perhaps even prohibited, even when they are occasions for luxury for someone. But it is also possible to imagine and to observe modes of behavior and ways of life that accommodate luxury just as well and further represent a desirable social enrichment. Disregarding the markedly diverse views people may take in evaluating a specific action, it is still the case that with a phenomenological description of luxury, we enter into a relationship to the criticism and justification of the phenomenon that is known in other reception aesthetics. When, say, Hans Ulrich Gumbrecht describes the way sports facilitate aesthetic

A special aesthetic experience **117**

experiences that intensify a sense of being, and goes on to make grand statements *In Praise of Athletic Beauty*, he is not praising specific sports practices at all, in fact these are not even under consideration. To give an example, if someone had the kind of aesthetic experience Gumbrecht describes while watching a horse race, neither he nor Gumbrecht is thereby either defending or endorsing the morally questionable ways animals are treated in many horse races. That is the parallel. Many athletes achieve exceptional aesthetic experiences and facilitate them for audiences only with the help of repugnant doping practices. Many people have experiences of luxury with things they acquired on the basis of despicable business practices and repellent egotism. Surely both should be evaluated in the same way. But in either case, the people in question can only be meaningfully reproached for their respective actions—not for having had these potentially aesthetic experiences.

## Without purpose: nonpurposeful and unpurposeful

A person who wants to experience luxury belongs to a group of people who fulfill two conditions. First, they must want to escape the pressure to be practical and correct; second, they must still be prepared and willing to break with common understandings, customary practices and social niceties. The last is just as necessary as the first. One who is not prepared to break with expectations and decorum will not be able to have the experience of luxury, however much he may long for emancipation. This does not mean that subversive eccentricity of any kind will lead to this experience, however. The key point is that a break with the ordinary, a protest against social demands, occurs in an act of nonconformity experienced as luxury in a very specific way: Namely, by means of a thing which is not purposeful. Not through, say, acts of revenge or violence, or through immoral actions, but solely by means of a defiant attempt to be unreasonable in a reasonable way, by taking a willfully exaggerated amount of trouble with regard to one's own possession. And that means that anyone who wants the experience of luxury must be prepared to use something that is not purposeful, that is, not suited to its purpose. The experience of luxury is a special form of an experience of a purpose without purposefulness. There is an analytical basis for this, for if

**118** The Dadaism of possession

something is associated with an exaggerated and nonpurposeful effort, this thing can no longer be suited to its purpose. But a thing can do exactly this—fulfill a purpose without being purposeful—in two ways: By being nonpurposeful and by being unpurposeful.

An excess of effort is nonpurposeful if an ordinary object works just as well with far less effort. To say it simply: Exaggerated effort in this case produces no loss and no gain in functionality. A terrazzo floor is far more difficult to produce than a laminate floor, for example, but there is no detectable difference between them in terms of walking on one or the other. They fulfill their function equally well, even if more than a few would say one of the two is decidedly more beautiful. But whether something is beautiful is irrelevant to the question of whether it is luxury.

The situation is completely different when an excess of effort leads to the thing being diminished in its functionality. In this case something is unpurposeful, even compared with something useful for the same purpose, despite far more effort having been expended than is necessary; one might easily have had a more suitable object with less effort. So, say, a clock with an elaborate enamel face is usually nonpurposeful for just that reason, for it does not function better or worse than a clock with a simpler printed face. A complicated mechanical watch can be unpurposeful, however, for despite being lavish in its manufacture, construction and requirements for care, it is ordinarily not nearly so practical, stable, precise or dependable as many simpler watches.

The difference between being *nonpurposeful with excessive effort* on the one hand and *unpurposeful with excessive effort* on the other, leads to the question of whether the refusal to be fit for purpose in a luxury object must occur in one of these two ways or could be possible in both. The question goes, specifically: Is the luxury good—that is, a thing that fulfills *a purpose without being purposeful*—an object that fulfills its purpose *nonpurposefully as a result of excessive effort* or an object that fulfills its purpose unpurposefully *as a result of excessive effort*? The remarkable thing about this possibly strange-sounding question is not only that it has a systematic relevance, but also that it is of interest from the standpoint of the history of philosophy, for it was Kant who answered it clearly.

A special aesthetic experience **119**

Kant continues to astonish, in his philosophical work, luxury hardly appears as a theme at all. Yet, when he says something about it in passing, he manages one of the most original—and possibly also the most radical—definitions of luxury to be found in all of philosophy. The reference is to a sentence fragment from the *Critique of Judgment*—this time from the second, less well-read part, however. In a long sentence of multiple clauses, Kant adds a bracket. In it, he suggests that "the culminating point ... where devotion to what is superfluous begins to be prejudicial to what is indispensable, is called luxury."[36] That implies that for Kant, the superfluous, dispensable effort that characterizes luxury goods works to the detriment of necessary, indispensable qualities. Only when such damage is done are we dealing with luxury. Luxury is, accordingly, just those objects that fulfill a purpose unpurposefully as a result of excessive effort. Just as some say dinosaurs made their lives more and more difficult as their size increased, so luxury goods' increasing complexity impairs their efficiency. For Kant, a luxury good is unnecessary, impractical and self-destructive; so the use of luxury goods has to have something uncomfortable, exhausting and complicated about it. Applied to one example, that means that a terrazzo floor could not be a luxury for the possessor, despite the mad effort of making it. For it achieves that which is indispensable for a floor covering very well, without any complications or negative effects. The enormous effort of making it in no way detracts from the functionality of using it. So, however large, impractical, irrational and superfluous it may be, for Kant it would never lead to calling such a floor a luxury.

As radical and original as Kant's way of looking at luxury is, it has the disadvantage of declaring an extreme case of luxury to be the only possible case. For Kant defends an objective concept of luxury—in sharp contrast to his description of beauty. An example shows this: A clock produced with a great deal of unnecessary effort could not be a luxury in Kant's view, despite functioning perfectly. But a clock made with unnecessary effort that starts to malfunction is luxury. What follows from this view is that a technician—in this case a clockmaker— can measure, test and so determine what luxury is. That means that the same object could not possibly be luxury for one person and not for another at the same time. And anyone who starts from the premise that this could be the case will struggle with Kant's concept of luxury.

**120** The Dadaism of possession

The situation actually looks completely different if, reception-aesthetically, one takes into account the effect the way the thing made with such exaggerated effort affects its possessor—as Kant did with beauty. From this perspective, the difference between *nonpurposeful with exaggerated effort* and *unpurposeful with exaggerated effort* plays no part. We would happily agree with Kant that one can have a particularly clear and radical experience of luxury from unpurposeful things produced with exaggerated effort. For here, the impracticality announces itself to the possessor in its use, appearing as a voluntarily and foolishly adopted self-impediment, like an unnecessary resistance. In such exceptionally clear instances of luxury one could—paradoxical as it sounds—speak of *opaque luxury*, to be distinguished from *transparent luxury*. This is encountered in things that are unpurposeful as a result of exaggerated effort. For in using an object that is merely nonpurposeful, no one would notice that it lacks purposefulness; superfluity is not perceptible and so is in this sense transparent. The possessor has to know about this purposelessness—yet it changes nothing about the last decisive point. Even this knowledge permits an experience of transgression with the thing; even an object whose exaggerated, silly extravagance is transparent can be possessed in order to use it to dadaistically resist demands for reasonable restraint, shrewd efficiency and astute practicality. This is the reason the concept of luxury should, from a phenomenological perspective, unlike Kant's, be grasped in such a way that an object that fulfills a purpose *nonpurposefully* because of exaggerated effort makes transparent luxury possible, and an object that fulfills a purpose *inefficiently* because of exaggerated effort makes opaque luxury possible. For both permit a possessor to have an experience of transgression.

## Two forms of transgression: inadequacy and excess

Boundaries may be overstepped in two directions—this also applies to conceptions of appropriate possession and appropriate effort. One may surpass these conceptions by way of a *too much* or fall short of them by way of a *too little*—and since it is about a break in both cases, it is not surprising that the effect on the person making the break is, or can be, comparable. For example, on many occasions too much effort in one's choice of clothing is as much of a break with conventions,

A special aesthetic experience **121**

expectations and customs as too little effort. But that would mean that if luxury is defined exclusively by the quality of the experience of autonomy that comes from a deliberate departure from expectations, then this experience of luxury could be achieved equally well by deliberately falling short. Christian Graf von Krockow, in his book *Die Heimkehr zum Luxus* [Luxury Comes Home] of 1989, takes this view, in fact, he sees in it the actual form of luxury. Speaking of a prosperous man who wears worn and patched clothing on any occasion, appropriate or not, he writes: "It suggests that he is noticeably falling short of what is usual, generally acceptable. At the same time, the luxurious quality is unmistakable" (tr.).[37] Krockow makes an original argument using the double meaning of the phrase, *being able to afford something*, which means both that one is in a position to get along without something, and that one is in a position to buy something. For Krockow, luxury is associated with the first meaning only. Someone who can permit himself a break with convention and goes on to do it is living in luxury as a result. Apart from whether his approach is excessively fastidious or excessively slovenly, in both cases he can say of himself: "I don't need these conventions, I can afford to break with them" (tr.).[38]

Falling short of the usual effort and exceeding it are two dissimilar sisters of the transgression against instrumentalism. For utilitarianism, functionalism and instrumentalism are always defined by the idea that there are suitable, which is to say efficient, solutions that take neither more nor less effort than is necessary. A preference for luxury and a preference for falling short have a basic refusal of utilitarian thinking in common. One can agree unreservedly with Max Weber, who defined luxury very much in this sense as an attitude. In *Economy and Society* of 1921, he understands "'Luxury' in the sense of rejecting purposive-rational control of consumption."[39]

What must be said of Krockow also applies to Weber: Luxury is the product of a rejecting, defiant attitude, but not every form of rejection of a utilitarian orientation to use leads to luxury. As persuasive as Krockow's descriptions are, it can hardly make sense to describe such deliberate inadequacy as, say, the patched suit, as luxury, despite the structural affinity between resulting experiences and this on simple grounds of definition. By the concept of luxury we mean nonpurposeful and exaggerated effort alone, not unsuitable effort of

**122** The Dadaism of possession

any kind. That means, in turn, that the concept of luxury specifies *one of two* possible kinds of refusal and overstepping of boundaries, namely the break with expectation by means of an exaggerated and nonpurposeful excess of effort only. It is not the one who comes to the ball in his patched suit who is wearing luxury, but the one who makes an unreasonable effort concerning his wardrobe, who, for example, has his suit specially made by a designer. If we were to include falling short of the usual effort in what we call luxury, the necessary characteristic for luxury would no longer be in place and the concept would be broadly synonymous with any deviation from the appropriate effort. In *Elements of the Philosophy of Right*, Hegel addresses this problem:

> Diogenes, in his whole character as a Cynic, is in fact merely a product of the social life of Athens, and what determined him was the opinion against which his entire way of life reacted. His way of life was therefore not independent, but merely a consequence of these social conditions, and itself an unprepossessing product of luxury.[40]

It is actually worth noting that at least the German language knows no separate concept for Hegel's "unprepossessing product of luxury"—that is, for things and behavior people use to thwart expectations through deliberate, nonconformist inadequacy. One could speak of a negative or an inverse luxury, different from positive luxury—as we would have to call it by analogy—in its apparent strategy, but possibly not in its phenomenal quality of experience for the possessor. The concept of asceticism is, in any case, not appropriate for negative luxury. For an ascetic does not normally intend to fall short of recognized levels of suitability, but rather does not believe in the validity of such a standard for the appropriate effort; as a result, it is as difficult for him to have an experience of transgression by means of negative luxury as it would be for someone suffering delusions of grandeur to have an experience of transgression by means of positive luxury. Generally speaking, someone who considers a small amount of effort to be nonpurposeful cannot defiantly fall short of the boundary, any more than someone who considers the greatest effort to be normal can overstep it.

## Luxury and rarity

Whatever terms we use for transgressions by overstepping and by falling short, they have one thing in common: Neither form functions on the basis of a *rarity* of the means employed, although one could certainly take this view, at least at first glance. The thesis would then be: Since utilitarian thinking in the managed world leads to mass production, the means of transgression and aesthetic liberation must exclude this instrumental rationality. That is, if luxury goods are a means of transgression, they must be things that are as unusual, rare or unique as possible. One encounters this idea in various places; in Arnold Gehlen's lecture "Luxus und Gesellschaft," [Luxury and Society], given in 1968, in which rarity turns into a proper definition of luxury:

> The objective characteristics of luxury goods consist of their being improbable, whether it be in quality, in quantity — Carl Theodor had 1000 horses, Graf Brühl in Dresden had 1500 wigs — or in their being exceptional, as were assembled in art — and curiosity cabinets (tr.).[41]

Hans Magnus Enzensberger argued in a similar way in his essay "Luxury: Where Does it Come From and Where is it Going?" of 1995, likewise equating luxury with something rare and from this— again as Gehlen did—developing a defense of the true and authentic luxury of the future. For that which is, in his view, usually treated as luxury is not rare at all, and is therefore only a false pseudoluxury:

> Under the sign of sprawling consumerism, fast cars and gold watches, cases of champagne and perfume, things available on every street corner are not scarce, rare, expensive and enviable. These are rather basic living conditions like peace, good water and enough space (tr.).[42]

With Gehlen, the analogous move from the rarity of luxury to genuine and true luxury goods is stated as:

> Now in general, we live in a time when life opportunities are narrowing. The horizons are not open, there is no doubt about

**124** The Dadaism of possession

> overpopulation, the best one can hope for is that things will not get worse, a widespread fractiousness betrays an absence of optimism and open vistas. The real meaning of luxury is the reverse, a bursting of constraints, an increase in life possibilities (tr.).[43]

It actually must be said that this conclusion about the time, peace, possibilities for experience and certainty as the real luxury goods in an overpopulated utilitarian society would be persuasive if the premises were persuasive, namely that luxury had to be something rare, scarce or improbable. But neither the history of the concept nor methodological reasoning is enough to construct a congruity or even a partial identity. Very rare books by completely unknown and forgotten authors can be found in any secondhand bookshop, but cannot be interpreted as luxury books just because they are rare. In the same way, the increasing difficulty of getting peace, security, space and time does not justify considering these things luxuries; however desirable they may be, they don't become luxuries for that reason alone. For luxury is bound up with an irrationally overblown possession. Such a thing does not become better or more reasonable if it is observed often or very rarely. A shoe made by hand continues to be a shoe made with great, perhaps superfluous effort, even if such a shoe is not a rarity in the shopping arcades of a metropolis. Just as a false argument is not corrected by repetition, a wasteful, complicated and superfluous thing does not become a modest, simple and necessary thing through repetition or high circulation. It is possible to resist the pressure to conform to standards of suitability through the possession of mass-produced goods. It is exaggerated, irrational, excessive effort that is a quality of luxury goods, not rarity. In their desire for rare things and events, however, people do sometimes have to make an exaggerated effort. That does not apply to an ordinary but rare book by a forgotten author in the secondhand shop. It does apply to a car with a motor that was constructed specially—one of a few ever made—which is unnecessarily difficult to use just because of its rarity, and furthermore exceptionally impractical and problematic for ordinary use. In such a case—but by no means in every case—rarity figures in the decision to consider the car luxurious.

A special aesthetic experience **125**

## Why luxury? Social pressure

Luxury is—as Max Weber writes—the product "of rejecting purposive-rational control of consumption."[44] There is widespread agreement that he is right about this. But views and interests diverge when we consider what to do next with this finding, what further questions should be asked. So it is possible to specify, as we just tried to do, that it makes sense to call this refusal of utilitarian orientation luxury only if it arises from too much and not from too little effort; we can further confirm that too much effort does not necessarily involve rarity of effort. With these specifications we are still concerned with the thing itself; we are trying to specify characteristics of the phenomenon. But sociologists, in particular, appear to be dissatisfied with an exclusively phenomenological description. At least there is evidence that they raise pointed questions about how luxury comes to be: Where does this refusing and defiant attitude of luxury with respect to instrumental reason come from? What are the reasons for someone deliberately overstepping expectations of restraint? In short: "Why is luxury and what is it for?" When it comes to answering these questions, what prevails is anything but unity. At least two classical answers will be set out, which could not themselves be more contradictory: One makes *social pressure*, and the other *longing for freedom* responsible for the rejection of instrumental logic.

The first answer is to be found in a particularly clear and succinct form in Max Weber—we need only finish reading the sentence cited earlier from *Economy and Society*: "Luxury is ... for the dominant feudal strata nothing superfluous: it is a means of social self-assertion."[45] Here is a figure of thought that works with the distinction between appearance and reality: Luxury appears to be something superfluous at first glance, something people choose voluntarily; if asked, they would say so. But despite this appearance, and although the people themselves think so, the refusal of instrumental rationality is in reality a product of social expectations and necessities. Each such person is actually forced into the wastefulness of luxury through their social group, level or class—whatever one would like to call this entity—even though the pressure cannot be seen, even if the people themselves don't believe that it is the case. Some social levels don't merely appreciate the wastefulness of luxury as a sign of their

**126** The Dadaism of possession

purchasing power, but also expect it; it gets to the point of making the waste necessary to ensure the cohesion of the group. One could almost sympathize. These people, who are in fact forced to appear wasteful, feel themselves sacrificed to the pressure of social expectation and are unhappy. Karl Marx made fun of the unfortunate capitalists in this sense in *Das Kapital* of 1867. Because they are—despite being ruled by "the most sordid avarice" according to Marx—actually required by society to waste, against their inclinations, and, against their will, to accumulate.

> When a certain stage of development has been reached, a conventional degree of prodigality which is also an exhibition of wealth, and consequently a source of credit, becomes a business necessity to the "unfortunate" capitalist. Luxury enters into capital's expenses of representation.[46]

For Weber and Marx, all these are largely short asides in which they make observations about luxury. Thorstein Veblen is undoubtedly the most important representative of such answers to the question of how the refusal of instrumental rationality by means of luxury comes to be. The whole argument of his famous book *The Theory of the Leisure Class* of 1899 stands or falls on there being no difference between luxury and ostentation. For Veblen, however, this lack of differentiation is neither an irritating omission nor even an understandable slovenliness, but the inevitable result of basic anthropological conviction. Veblen is typical of many who despise luxury in exactly this respect. Put concisely, the view of Weber, Marx and Veblen states: *There are not and cannot be any Dadaists.* Because for them the critique of luxury—and especially the thought figure that distinguishes between appearance and reality—is the inevitable result of their belief, in principle, that people would not willingly do something consciously irrational, wasteful and superfluous. If someone possesses a watch with an extremely complicated construction that does not function especially well despite the enormous effort it took to make it, then they would see this person, with his superfluous possession, either as pursuing a hidden purpose, or as having been forced into possessing it, or even both. For according to Veblen, the cultural life of human beings is determined by those utilitarian, instrumental

A special aesthetic experience **127**

principles described by Charles Darwin—and Darwinism is known to be harsh on luxuriating: "The life of man in society, just like the life of other species, is a struggle for existence, and therefore it is a process of selective adaptation."[47] Since deliberate wastefulness, just like leisure, is unnecessary and irrational for Veblen, for him there must always be a hidden, deeper, authentic, secret purpose or force that finally makes this wastefulness something rational and utilitarian after all. But Veblen—like most critics of luxury—believes he knows best about this inconspicuous, hidden purpose in what is without purpose. This is primarily because for him there is *a priori* only one reason. Human beings are wasteful and leisurely only because this is a way to demonstrate their own capacity to spend or because their business situation expects it of them.

For this thought figure, which is very widespread among sociologists in particular, examples are easy to find. In *Distinction* of 1979, Pierre Bourdieu defined "luxury, as the manifestation of the distance from necessity."[48] Such a short aside is sufficient to express the critical thing: Bourdieu does not link luxury to the distance from the sphere of necessity that a person actually experiences, if perhaps does not demonstrate. From a phenomenological standpoint it is an unsatisfactory and irritating simplification. For a person can *experience* a distance to the sphere of the necessary personally and privately, as well as *demonstrate* a distance to the sphere of the necessary outwardly with symbols. But these are two fundamentally different phenomena that may not be tossed into the same pot. Someone could symbolically fake a distance to the sphere of the necessary without ever having experienced it himself. Conversely, a person can experience a distance to the sphere of the necessary himself without having to demonstrate it openly. But this critical difference cannot be grasped as long as luxury is defined sociologically as *display with possessions* and not phenomenologically as *experience with possessions*. What follows from the sociological view is clear: One's own experience, in the way it is given from the perspective of the first person singular, must be absolutely irrelevant. Formulated in another way, the basic, implicitly given, anthropological assumption—*there are no Dadaists*—leads inevitably to a reduction that no longer fairly represents the phenomena, that is, the variety of both luxury as it is experienced as well as ostentation as it is displayed in people's lives. A conceptual differentiation between

**128** The Dadaism of possession

*luxury* and *ostentation* is—for Veblen, just as for Bourdieu—not simply unnecessary, but impossible. As soon as the level of experience is bracketed out of a sociological view of luxury, as soon as luxury is thought to be a symbol or a kind of exposition, exaggerated, impractical consumption can no longer be considered deliberately silly or defiant, but has to be a utilitarian status symbol—namely unmistakable "evidence of wealth"[49]—because otherwise there would be no such thing. So the sociological view is that this is the only way either form of transgression of instrumental activity—for Veblen demonstrative consumption and demonstrative leisure—can be understood.

Identifying luxury with ostentation puts us in a properly paradoxical situation. What we set out to criticize finally, inevitably, ceases to exist. At that point it no longer makes sense to speak of a critique of luxury. Weber, Marx or Veblen do not deny a positive value for luxury, that is, but rather deny that it exists at all. For them, luxury's existence is specious. In reality, as Weber writes, the superfluous is "nothing 'superfluous'"[50]; in reality, as Marx writes, waste is an essential "cost of representing capital"[51]; in reality, as Veblen writes, "the consumption of finer goods is evidence of wealth"[52] made "for this purpose."[53] As a result, the concept *prestige* is always understood as something sustained through "standards of good repute."[54] From this standpoint, then, there isn't really any voluntary expenditure or pointless waste. Here, the critics are not just criticizing luxury, but seeking to destroy any aspiration to luxury by trying to prove that luxury is actually the very thing they don't want to be: Utilitarian, efficient and rational instruments. In his lecture "Veblen's Attack on Culture" of 1941, Theodor W. Adorno saw through this kind of argument in a particularly perceptive and precise way, pointing out that it denies the existence of luxury by means of a supposition that cannot be proven.

Adorno shows himself to be well and truly incensed about Veblen's attempt to present the whole of culture as sham and lies. He describes in detail how Veblen's argument—even if Veblen doesn't say it explicitly—supports the thesis that "Culture turns against utility for the sake of a mediated utility."[55] Yet, if this thesis were true, for Adorno it would be a repulsive, disgusting diagnosis, unacceptable because it effectively implies that culture "is marked by a life-lie."[56] Adorno becomes particularly incensed about people being denied the very possibility of thinking they might be capable of resisting the utilitarian rationality of an administrated world, one that extends into the

## A special aesthetic experience **129**

banalities of everyday life. Someone who takes his own apartment to be luxury on the basis of its size and furnishings is deluding himself, because in fact he knows that with this apartment he is actually only doggedly submitting to social pressure for self-presentation. Adorno delivers a distinctly harsh verdict of Veblen. At points one gets the impression that Adorno considers this interpretation of luxury to come close to a pathology, fueled by irrational fears and malicious assumptions. But Adorno is perfectly correct in his verdict, that Veblen, this "cultural efficiency expert,"[57] almost hysterically takes each and every thing he finds unnecessary to be a product of a rampant, secret, dangerous compulsion to waste. Think of a simple floral carpet: "In Veblen's eyes, the ornamentation becomes menacing ..."[58]

Perhaps the severity of Adorno's critique can be explained by his having seen what Veblen's view—if also Marx's, Weber's and Bourdieu's—puts in question: That the dispute about luxury, as a phenomenon *sui generis*, is in fact a dispute about the existence of an autonomous and idiosyncratic subject. Now, Adorno is known to be the last to overlook the massive social threat this autonomous subject is facing. But as much as this threat infuriates him, he is no less infuriated when the possibility of transgression, of resistance, of "emancipation from the realm of utility"[59] is simply interpreted away. For despite all the negativism that characterizes his philosophy, Adorno recognizes a subject's capacity to resist being taken in by a functionalized society. If we are not at least able to think that people could resist the dictates of instrumental reason—through luxury or by other means, perhaps education or art—then luxury must be identified as pretense. But that finally means that "all of culture becomes for him the meaningless ostentatious display of the bankrupt."[60] For Adorno, this is a *reductio ad absurdum*. If a "glorification of a Darwinian struggle for existence"[61] makes it impossible to even think about the existence of culture, the position is absurd—and furthermore dangerous: "To be consistent, he [Veblen] would have to demand that art be eliminated."[62]

## Notes

1  Martin Seel, "Ästhetik und Aisthetik" in Birgit Recki and Lambert Wiesing, eds., *Bild und Reflexion, Paradigmen und Perspektiven der gegenwärtigen Ästhetik* (Munich: Wilhelm Fink, 1997), 28.

**130** The Dadaism of possession

2 Immanuel Kant, *Critique of Judgement*, trans. James Creed Meredith, revised by Nicolas Walker (Oxford: Oxford University Press, 2007) §2, 37.
3 ibid., §16, 62.
4 ibid., §5, 41.
5 Seel, "Ästhetik und Aisthetik," 29.
6 ibid., 34.
7 ibid., 32.
8 Kant, *Critique of Judgment*, §23, 76.
9 ibid., §9, 49.
10 ibid., §23, 75.
11 ibid., §1, 36.
12 ibid., §1, 35.
13 Seel, "Ästhetik und Aisthetik," 31.
14 Ullrich, *Habenwollen*, 29.
15 Erich Fromm, *To Have or to Be* (London and New York: Continuum, 1997 [1976]), 79.
16 Kant, *Critique of Judgment*, §25, 80.
17 Walter Benjamin, "Unpacking My Library: A Talk about Book Collecting," in Hannah Arendt, ed., *Illuminations*, trans. Harry Zohn (New York: Schocken, 1969), 59–60.
18 ibid., 60.
19 ibid.
20 ibid., 67.
21 Ullrich, *Habenwollen*, 190.
22 Theodor W. Adorno, *Theorie der Halbbildung* (Frankfurt/M.: Suhrkamp, 2006 [1959]), 16.
23 Moritz Geiger, *Zugänge zur Ästhetik* (Leipzig: Der neue Geist, 1928), 46.
24 Ullrich, *Habenwollen*, 185 f.
25 Wolfgang Ullrich, "Besitzen statt rezipieren: Wie die Ikonographie zeitgenössischer Kunstsammler die Ideale moderner Kunst revidiert," in *Pop. Kultur & Kritik* 5 (2014), 125.
26 ibid., 122 f.
27 Peter Sloterdijk, *Not Saved: Essays after Heidegger*, trans. Ian Alexander Moore and Christopher Turner (Cambridge: Polity Press, 2017 [2001]), 122.
28 An idea that stands at the center of reflections by Robert Pfaller; see: *Wofür es sich zu leben lohnt: Elemente materialistischer Philosophie,* [Why Living is Worthwhile: Elements of Materialist Philosophy] (Frankfurt/M.: Fischer, 2011).
29 Georg Friedrich Wilhelm Hegel, *Philosophie des Rechts: Die Vorlesung von 1819/20 in einer Nachschrift* (Frankfurt/M.: Suhrkamp, 1983), 155.
30 Friedrich Schiller, *On the Aesthetic Education of Man in a Series of Letters*, trans. Elizabeth M. Wilkinson and L.A. Willoughby, eds., (Oxford: Clarendon Press, 2005 [1795]) "14th Letter," 95.
31 Kurt Schwitters, "Brief vom 24.7.1946 an Christof Spengemann" in Ernst Nündel, eds., *Wir Spielen, bis uns der Tod abholt: Briefe aus fünf Jahrzehnten* (Frankfurt/M., Berlin and Vienna: Ullstein, 1974), 211.

A special aesthetic experience **131**

32 Carl Laszlo, "Bevor Neo-Dada da war, war Dada da" in *Aufruf zum Luxus und Andere Manifeste* (Stuttgart: Collispress Paul Eckhardt, 1967 [1966]) np.
33 Carl Laszlo, "Aufruf zum Luxus" in *Aufruf zum Luxus und Andere Manifeste* (Stuttgart: Collispress Paul Eckhardt, 1967 [1960]), np.
34 ibid.
35 ibid.
36 Kant, *Critique of Judgment*, §83, 261.
37 Christian Graf von Krockow, *Die Heimkehr zum Luxus: Von der Notwendigkeit des Überflussigen* (Zurich: Kreuz, 1989), 7.
38 ibid.
39 Max Weber, *Economy and Society: An Outline of Interpretive Sociology*, trans. Guenther Roth and Claus Wittich (Berkeley, Los Angeles and London: University of California Press, 1978 [1921]), 1106.
40 Georg Wilhelm Friedrich Hegel, *Elements of the Philosophy of Right*, trans. H.B. Nisbet (Cambridge: Cambridge University Press, 1991 [1821]), §195, 231.
41 Arnold Gehlen, "Luxus und Gesellschaft" in Karl-Siegbert Rehberg, ed., *Die Seele im technischen Zeitalter und andere soziologische Schriften und Kulturanalysen* (Frankfurt/M.: Vittorio Klostermann, 2004 [1968]), 529–541536.
42 Hans Magnus Enzensberger, "Luxus: woher, und wohin damit? Reminiszenzen an den Überfluß" in Hans Magnus Enzensberger, ed., *Zickzack, Aufsätze* (Frankfurt/M.: Suhrkamp, 1997 [1995]), 157.
43 Gehlen, "Luxus und Gesellschaft," 539.
44 Weber, *Economy and Society*, 1106.
45 Weber, *Economy and Society*, 1106.
46 Karl Marx, *Capital: A Critique of Political Economy*, ol. 1, trans. Samuel Moore and Edward Aveling (Moscow: Progress Publishers, 2015 [1867]), 418.
47 Thorstein Veblen, *The Theory of the Leisure Class* (Oxford: Oxford University Press, 2007 [1899]), 125.
48 Bourdieu, Pierre, *Distinction: A Social Critique of the Judgment of Taste*, trans. Richard Nice (Cambridge: Harvard University Press, 1984 [1979]), 254.
49 Veblen, *Leisure Class*, 49.
50 Weber, *Economy and Society*, 1106.
51 Marx, *Capital*, 418.
52 Veblen, *Leisure Class*, 53.
53 ibid.
54 ibid.,152.
55 Theodor W. Adorno, "Veblen's Attack on Culture" in *Prisms*, trans. Samuel Weber and Shierry Weber (Cambridge: MIT Press, 1981 [1941]), 76.
56 ibid.
57 ibid.
58 ibid., 78.
59 ibid., 75.
60 ibid.
61 ibid.,93.
62 ibid., 86, n. 3.

# 5

# WHY LUXURY?

## Why luxury? The longing for freedom

Against the background of his critique of Veblen, it is not surprising that Adorno himself—as well as his student Bazon Brock—gives a completely different answer to the question about why someone would consciously transgress against expectations to be reasonable. To the satisfaction of any phenomenologist, Adorno answers this question in a way that takes the first person perspective of the possessor seriously and that rules out any kind of explanation by means of supposition. The rejection of a utilitarian orientation toward use, Adorno says, arises from the simple wish for a better life, for a better culture. As a reason for possessing a luxury, Adorno indicates a belief in a modernity that "has escaped the principle of unvarnished necessity and become humane."[1] There are passages, especially in the critique of Veblen, where one gets the impression that Adorno is using *luxury* and *culture* as synonyms. In his work as a whole, however, one rather gets the impression that *luxury* is often being equated with *life*. At least the central statement that Adorno formulated about life in *Minima Moralia* of 1951 supports luxury without reservation. In fact his description of life uses luxury as an essential feature: "If a life fulfilled its vocation directly, it would miss it."[2] That is the common ground between life and luxury. If luxury fulfilled a purpose in a straightforward way, it would not achieve the thing that defines it: The experience of a subject's idiosyncrasy in a function-dominated world. The

## Why luxury? **133**

experience of luxury, like the successful, happy life—one could include education as well—cannot be understood in functional terms, because these phenomena go beyond serving a function. A successful, happy human life only occurs when it is—like a luxury good—more than just a means to an end. One can only speak of an educated person if his knowledge is more comprehensive than is necessary for the practice of his profession. So for Adorno, luxury always has something human about it and conversely, a human life always has something luxurious. In the appendix of *Minima Moralia* he writes of human relationships: "Any that is really human takes on an aspect of luxury in the realm of utility" (tr.).[3] A good life, that is, is more than a life for the sake of efficiently serving a purpose. There is a structural affinity between the quality of a human life and the quality of luxury—and that is exactly why Veblen's position is so humanly dangerous for Adorno. In Adorno's view, both luxury and human life would be absolutely destroyed if life were reduced to an existence that is no more than an efficient means to an end. For him, luxury and human life are threatened by the same enemy: Namely by the dominance of instrumental reason alone. One could also say, from Adorno's point of view, luxury is necessary for a good life, for otherwise this life is reduced to utilitarian rationality.

With these reflections we can understand why Adorno's description of luxury in his critique of Veblen is supported by an equally simple, perhaps also unrealistic, hope for a better, sociable and happy life. Bazon Brock takes this hope up by explicitly understanding and defending "luxuriating as a social strategy" (tr.),[4] as a contribution to a more humane world. For Adorno, as for Brock, when we are concerned with luxury we are concerned with the improvement of society. It is astonishing how openly the reason for rejecting the utilitarian orientation toward use is represented as a personal perception, or at least a completely private feeling. Adorno speaks of the "yearning to escape the enslavement to utility."[5] That there is such yearning among human beings, Adorno is certain. But not, say, because he has asked people. His argument for the existence of longing is finally circular: The existence of luxury is said to show that there is a longing; that there is luxury rests on the existence of this longing. If this longing were not the driving motivation for luxury, then transgression would be not luxury but—as it is for Veblen—vile ostentation.

**134** The Dadaism of possession

## Luxury and art

The longing to escape the slavery of goals is Adorno's reason for identifying luxury as a willful subject's reply to a world dominated by utility. But, for Adorno, this longing has several children, not to say that luxury has a twin sister: Art. And this is what is astonishing. In his lecture on Veblen at the beginning of the 1940s, Adorno attributed the same utopian power and meaning to luxury that he used 30 years later, in *Aesthetic Theory*, to define art. There is no need to read far into *Aesthetic Theory* for what Adorno says about the special power of resistance art has against every kind of social submission. His view, on the very first page, corresponds to his interpretation of Veblen's view of luxury, except that he is speaking of art rather than luxury: "All efforts to restore art by giving it a social function—of which art in itself is uncertain and by which it expresses its own uncertainty—are doomed."[6]

Even in the formulations, one can detect that for Adorno art at least partly assumes the social function of luxury. The famous formulation of the "double character of art"[7] is preceded by the "double character of luxury."[8] From the "dialectic of luxury"[9] comes the "dialectic of artworks."[10] This is not at all to suggest that everything Adorno said of art he would have said of luxury as well. This is only about the opposite idea: Adorno finds established characteristics of luxury in art. The most important common ground may be that for Adorno, we are dealing in both cases with objects that permit special experiences because they are not crude, efficient instruments: "Artworks"—in fact Adorno could have said luxury goods—"are plenipotentiaries of things that are no longer distorted by exchange, profit, and the false needs of a degraded humanity."[11] Both phenomena emerge from the oppositional attitude of a willful subject. Art and luxury share the same longing: "a liberated society ... beyond the irrationality of its *faux frais* and beyond the ends-means-rationality of utility."[12] Adorno characterized luxury, as he did art, as an emancipatory intention, with which subjects—not in the same way, but to the same degree—defend themselves against a complete integration into a functionalized society. Despite all negativism, Adorno believed unreservedly that such autonomy and emancipation are possible. This very thing makes it more understandable that Adorno would find Veblen's

Why luxury? **135**

way of looking at luxury so infuriatingly cynical. What Veblen said about luxury could, after all, always be said about art as well. Furthermore, Veblen's way of looking at luxury as the product of hidden, repressed and authentic interests in status cannot be refuted; it has the form of a terminal argument, because it doesn't matter what a subject does. It can always be claimed that he's only behaving in a nonconformist and affirmative way because his real interests are hidden. With this argument it could also be said that atonal music is really just a commodity in the strict sense, as is jazz. Adorno is right, this is the way for a subject to lose the very possibility of asserting his autonomy. So he declares himself in favor of distinguishing just as strictly between ostentation and luxury as between the culture industry and art—remarkably, by the same argument.

That dialectical moment shared by art and luxury can be seen in their comparable relationship to society. Both luxury and art are, in Adorno's view, "part of the social product which does not serve human needs and contribute to human happiness."[13] But he also particularly emphasizes that this does not exhaust either art or luxury. People use both art and luxury to defend themselves against being caught and dehumanized by a system of pervasive utilitarian rationality. What Adorno first discovered in luxury later became a key feature of art for him:

> The other side of luxury is the use of parts of the social product which serve not the reproduction of extended labor, directly or indirectly, but of man in so far as he is not entirely under the sway of the utility principle.[14]

For Adorno, this may actually be the most important characteristic that luxury and art have in common: Their special way of opposing instrumental rationality. For neither art nor luxury sets out to be socially destructive or even socially revolutionary; the concepts being opposed are not explicitly fought against or consciously meant to be destroyed. Art and luxury do not oppose the utilitarian world directly. They propose none of their own alternatives, but rather just offer subjects the possibility of willfully withdrawing from it; it is about—as Adorno wrote with such phenomenological precision—"escaping the slavery of goals"; only that also means that it is not about ending the

**136** The Dadaism of possession

slavery of goals. This description usually matches the lifestyles of those with interests in art and luxury. At least it seems that people with interests in art and luxury do not, on the one hand, categorically reject social instrumentalism and utilitarianism, but, on the other hand, still do not want to be fully absorbed and defined by it. It is about a basic difference between supposing that art and luxury mean freeing, emancipating, releasing oneself from coercion, or wanting to destroy, do away with the coercion and replace it with something else. Adorno takes a clear and persuasive position on the issue: Aesthetic experiences—whether through art or through luxury—permit the first, but not the second. What Adorno writes about art in *Aesthetic Theory* applies without the slightest restriction to luxury: "Whereas art opposes society, it is nevertheless unable to take up a position beyond it; it achieves opposition only through identification with that against which it remonstrates."[15]

It is possible to pinpoint the common ground between luxury and art that Adorno does not himself make explicit, but that is to be found in his work. Luxury and art share, for Adorno, the same *neither-nor*. Both phenomena arise from the same balancing act: Luxury and art are to the same extent *neither* purposeless *nor* purposeful. Or to formulate it positively: Both phenomena arise from a rejection of purposefulness—yet the rejection is only possible if a purpose is being pursued. So for Adorno, luxury, as well as art, is unthinkable without a purpose. When something serves no purpose at all, we cannot speak of either an appropriate or an exaggerated effort. Luxury always develops from a thing with a purpose. That is why luxury is experienced only in that use which is possible for the possessor, that is, only when a luxurious thing is used for the purpose it serves with irrational effort in a nonpurposeful or unpurposeful way. Because what is the case for luxury is also what defines art: "That which is to be broken remains essential for the aesthetic break."[16] Both forms of transgression require "aesthetic purposefulness."[17] That has consequences. Since he is modelling art on luxury, Adorno must step forward as a vehement critic of the idea of *l'art pour l'art*, which he does. It is the example he uses to show that it is also possible to exaggerate desirable "emancipation from the realm of utility,"[18] so that they turn dialectically upside down, reversing emancipation from the realm of goals into sheer arbitrariness of purpose, empty ornamentation and absence of function.

Why luxury? **137**

Adorno is not even entirely sure, in light of the widespread proclamation of its absolute purposelessness, whether art still even exists. There need be no such fear with respect to luxury: "It is uncertain whether art is still possible; whether, with its complete emancipation, it did not sever its own preconditions."[19]

Adorno draws limits for art and luxury on two sides: Exactly, and in the same respect, as there was no luxury without purpose and no art without purpose, neither is there any purposeful art or purposeful luxury. Adorno explicitly describes two dangers, ways art can lose its crucial autonomous status by serving a purpose: Through *sensuality* and through *communication*. Here the parallels to luxury continue. For justice is not done to either phenomenon as long as they are considered "a higher order of amusement."[20] If an object fulfills the function of being sensuously enjoyable, it is something utilitarian and so neither luxury nor art: "Only once it has done with tasteful savouring does artistic experience become autonomous."[21] That does not mean, however, that objects referred to as art and as luxury cannot be sensual and comfortable as well. Various experiences are possible with one and the same object. But both the experience of art and the experience of luxury may be distinguished from the experience of sensual pleasure, in fact using the same indications. Luxury and art come from a familiarity and experience with an "opposition to society"[22] achieved by means of a thing—and the character of exactly this familiarity and experience of not-fitting-in is crucial: The dadaistic rejection of utilitarian orientation. Neither luxury nor art articulates the break with instrumental reason reasonably. Both phenomena, art and luxury, confront functionalized society to the same extent, without designing a new counter-ideology. Luxury's transgression, like that of art, "occurs through non-communication."[23] It is not described as an articulated oppositional position, but felt as an aesthetic experience of autonomy: "What is social in art is its immanent movement against society, not its manifest opinions."[24]

## Art: luxury without purpose

The wide-ranging identity between luxury and art found with Adorno must not deceive us into thinking we cannot define a difference that is as simple as it is clear: It is essential for luxury to be

**138** The Dadaism of possession

constituted with an object that has a specific, usually an everyday, purpose. Only something that is a means to an end can be experienced as luxury, that is, as a something that serves this purpose awkwardly and impractically, with inefficient, exaggerated effort. This description no longer applies to art. The special position of the work of art for Adorno is clear against the background of his understanding of luxury. To put it concisely, art is luxury without purpose. For a work of art is set apart for Adorno in that it actually attempts the impossible, namely to make it possible to experience the step—familiar from luxury—from the slavery of goals toward emancipation, through an object that has, in contrast to a luxury good, no recognizable instrumental purpose at all. If we compare Adorno's understanding of art with his understanding of luxury, we see that a work of art is a luxury reduced to its emancipatory effect. Art possesses only this effect of noncompliance; it is not at the same time a thing with an everyday purpose, producing this effect in being used for this purpose. A work of art is just as irrational, wasteful, inappropriate, dadaistic, contrary, nonconformist, not-instrumental, disavowing, defiant, unreasonable and defensive as luxury. A work of art is not interested in being comfortable, beautiful, pleasant, attractive, enjoyable, sensual, easy, satisfying, exciting or even merely entertaining, either. Like luxury, a work of art defends itself against every symbolic and communicative function— whether as a poster or as a pretense. In reading Adorno's *Aesthetic Theory* with this far-reaching commonality in the background, that is, with the background of his early essay on Veblen, *Aesthetic Theory* appears to be the great, hopeful outline of a vision that somehow a paradox is possible after all, namely, that in addition to the impure everyday luxury with a purpose, a pure, artistic form is possible and necessary: Luxury without a purpose. A work of art then—and for Adorno, *only* a work of art—can succeed in willfully contradicting the managed society and the managed life of human beings, although a work of art, in contrast to a luxury good, cannot be used for any ordinary purpose. The only purpose art must serve, then, consists in making it possible for a recipient to experience the emancipation from the realm of purposes that is known from luxury. But that means that the purpose of art consists in freeing luxury—purpose without purposefulness—from purpose. The idea of art, for Adorno, is *pure* nonpurposefullnes.

Why luxury? **139**

In short, we can say that according to Adorno—and this appears to be a really remarkable definition of art—art is people's willful attempt to make something that has the purpose of being a luxury for them without having to serve another purpose in order to do it, that is, without having to be usable for anything specific. The strength of this definition is clear: Luxury cannot be defined ontologically by characteristics of a material kind any more than art can be. Both come about by allowing a recipient to experience autonomy and liberation from rational contexts. The only difference between them is that art tries to achieve this with things that have no purpose and luxury with things that do.

This presents a problem, however. How can an art object that is not there to instrumentally serve an everyday purpose ever produce the effect characteristic of luxury, namely, to put itself beyond frameworks of efficiency and reason by being wasteful, defiant, inappropriate, irrational, exaggerated, unreasonable, extravagant, provocative or uneconomical? There would be good reason to consider it impossible. For a thing can only be exaggerated, inefficient, inappropriate, etc. on the condition that it has a purpose. But the conclusion in reverse means that if an art object serves no purpose, then this object cannot be interpreted as counter-efficient, irrational, provocative, etc.—unless someone buys the thing without a purpose for an exorbitant price. In fact, this appears to be not the only way, but one way, not rarely chosen in the art world, of permitting a recipient to have an experience of autonomy and emancipation from purposeful contexts. Think of a banal object or an arrangement of all sorts of things, of a boring and plain mass-produced thing, that has been declared to have no specific purpose and so to be a work of art. Although nothing about the thing's construction makes it exceptional, although the thing is neither provocative or in any other way wasteful or irrationally inappropriate, it nevertheless facilitates the remarkable experience, familiar from luxury as well, of putting oneself beyond frameworks of appropriateness and rational purpose by means of one's possession of this thing— of course, it is only a hook for the one who buys this object at an astronomical price.

We can observe an assimilation of art to luxury, grounded in the relationship between art and luxury: An art that is nothing but expensive needs to be received as luxurious. Traditional, contemplative

**140** The Dadaism of possession

observation becomes an unsuitable form of reception for an art that is not a work, that is not beautiful, that awakens no sense of recognition and is not sublime in any way, but rather is only expensive. An adequate exhibition venue is, accordingly, not an art museum but an art fair. But that does not mean that art that is merely expensive automatically becomes luxury just by virtue of its exorbitant price. On the contrary: Any thing can bring about experiences of autonomy and emancipation from rational frameworks for only one buyer through the payment of an irrational price. But no thing becomes a luxury good solely by way of an irrationally overblown price. In order to be able to speak meaningfully of a thing as luxury, exaggerated, irrational, impractical effort must still be given in the thing in the fulfillment of its purpose. That is a necessary condition! And a banal, plain object is simply *per definitionem* not an object associated with elaborate, to say nothing of exaggerated effort, not even if has been declared art and sold at a dadaistic price. But this difference in the thing does not rule out that in a society defined by a rampant utilitarian thinking, the special form of reception as luxury would gain in significance and attraction. If just-being-expensive becomes the sole reason something is considered art, then simple observation of the thing paradoxically no longer delivers the experience that is the basis for saying the thing is an art object. In this case, the thing must be possessed as a luxury—without being a luxury.

## Luxury and elegance

Emancipation from the realm of purposes through luxury is, in an aesthetic evaluation, a phenomenon of not being present. A thing is experienced as luxury if it is experienced, consciously and in a certain way, *not* to be something in particular—more specifically, that it is *not* practical because it demands so much effort. But that also means that a thing becomes a luxury when, and if, it is possible to perceive in it an *independence from determinants*—and this very description applies to the phenomenon of elegance. Once again, we are not concerned with the empirical content that surely qualifies many things to be both elegant and luxurious. The relationship is not one of content, but of structure. Luxury and elegance may be thought of as two aesthetic phenomena of independence or release, something

Why luxury? **141**

like the way overstepping or falling short of appropriate effort was described earlier as two complementary phenomena of the transgression of purposefulness. The idea is, in any case, that the elegant object has the same relationship to the reasons it came to be as the luxurious object has to the purposes that brought it about. In short, elegance behaves toward causes as luxury does toward purposes. In both cases, something frees itself aesthetically from the control the purposes otherwise respectively exert.

In contrast to the concept of luxury, the concept of elegance certainly has many expressions that are very similar, if not synonymous. Being elegant implies something like being poised, reserved and graceful. Whatever concept one may choose from the list, it always means that something appears to an observer to be free from causal links among things, which does not mean that it actually is free. From a physical standpoint, there is no elegance for things. For a physical object is only and always the result of physical causes. Everything material in the world is subject to the conditions of its material formation—which, however, does not rule out the possibility that some things might look *as if* the conditions did not apply. Elegance is such a phenomenon of reception or effect. The concept of elegance is an aesthetic category: It describes the way something physically works on someone's perception, as if physical laws had been suspended.

The aesthetic effect of the elegant object is known from the phenomenological theory of images—one can say that the unspoken model for all elegance is the image. The elegant object has the effect of an image object that has become real. No image object is considered a real, physical object, but rather a special, artificial object that is visible to the observer on a material support and is, in fact, only visible. An image object—a person seen on a piece of paper, for example—cannot be touched or smelled. Rather one sees something that is like a phantom: The things seen in the image do not change. And it is exactly for this reason that image objects, consisting of pure visibility, are elegant in principle. They do not participate in the causal relationships among things. It has to be said, in fact, that such elegant things as can be seen in images can be seen nowhere else. Looking at an image is like an emancipatory look into a physics-free zone. Only here can a person see something that is not part of the physical world in which he, as a human being, must live. In the world of physical things, however,

**142** The Dadaism of possession

elegance exists only as an as-if-phenomenon. Something looks *as if* it were free of physical constraints, although it is not: The elegant thing looks *as if* it were an image object.

In the celebrated essay *Über das Marionettentheater* [On the Marionette Theatre] of 1810, Heinrich von Kleist coined a new word especially for this as-if-phenomenon: Anti-grave. That is, something is elegant, graceful or poised because it appears to be independent and autonomous with respect to physics and the environment. Graceful or elegant marionettes "know nothing of the inertia of material, the quality that most effectively resists dance" (tr.).[25] Here the elegant object has the effect of an imaginary object free of the physical, as if it found itself at an elevated—Nietzsche would say, aristocratic—distance from mundane and ordinary events. Elegant things are of this world, as is everything physical, but they successfully hide this origin from perception.

The concept of elegance may be thought of more broadly and comprehensively than as aesthetic emancipation from the physical alone. In its appearance, the elegant object finally hides not only its material weight and the ongoing effect of the environment, but also its entire worldly genesis. That is, the elegant thing withholds from view not only its original causes, but also all the conditions that made it possible for it to be as it is. "The effect of elegance," as Honoré de Balzac describes it in his "Treatise on the Elegant Life," of 1830, "depends primarily on keeping the means employed hidden" (tr.).[26] This is especially true of means that are necessarily economic. So, whether an elegant object is made in a simple or complex way, it produces the effect of elegance by hiding its cheap or expensive origin, very much in the sense of the dictum *ars artem celandi*. In his *Cahiers*, Paul Valéry got to the heart of this broad understanding of art's elegance, extending it not only to the invisibility of technical-causal, but also financial conditions. In 1922, he noted:

> *Elegantia* — is freedom and economy, translated for the eye — ease and facility in — difficult things — Finding without giving the impression of having searched — Carrying without seeming to feel the weight, — Knowing, without showing what has been learnt — And, in short, managing to suppress the

Why luxury? **143**

appearance if not of reality, then of the price which precious things have extracted.[27]

For example, in his novel *Around the World in Eighty Days*, Jules Verne sketches the figure of a man who is always elegantly as well as luxuriously dressed—the gentleman and eccentric Phileas Fogg. In the course of his journey, Fogg lands in the most impossible situations. He fights his way through several jungles, travels across various deserts and savannahs and crosses many seas and rivers, not rarely by improvised means. None of it has the slightest effect on his flawless, perfect clothing—the harsh conditions leave no trace, whatever happens, Phileas Fogg is always neat as a pin. Whether it's shoes or stockings, everything is spotlessly clean—the white shirt is ironed with precision. There's never a thought of a mark or stain, or even wear, despite all the exertions. That is the point: Fogg's lily-white shirt is in fact linked into the causal chains of worldly things, but we can't see it in him, and that constitutes part of his aesthetic effect. The clothing, and in the end the person too, appears to have a protective coating that wards off not only rain, but physical forces of any sort. Fogg is impermeably genteel and elegant because he is free from the slavery of causality.

Against this background, the structural parallel emerges: Elegance appears as untouched by the *laws of physics* as luxury does from the *laws of utility*. They are both forms of displacement, nonparticipation, abstention; one could speak of a pause in participation, but this in response to different pressures in each case. For we are dealing with two complementary forms of aesthetic autonomy. The elegant appears to be autonomous because it cannot be constrained by physical causality—it sets itself *weightlessly* beyond it. The luxurious appears autonomous because it cannot be constrained by meaningful utility—it sets itself *dadaistically* beyond it, whereby the former necessarily determines the latter. For it is no random coincidence that Phileas Fogg's clothing is both elegant and luxurious. In fact, it offers a good way to demonstrate the inescapable intrinsic connection between the elegant and the luxurious.

Mr Fogg does not present himself in anything like practical, functional travel clothing. Although his clothes fulfill the general purpose of clothing, they do it with no thought for utility. A starched white

**144** The Dadaism of possession

shirt is not the appropriate, sensible, obvious thing for crossing a jungle. The clothing is luxurious because it is uncomfortable, complicated and impractical. Anyone who wears such shirts in the jungle is deliberately setting himself beyond rational, utilitarian thinking. *That is, to be elegant in the jungle is a luxury.* And that may be generalized to the jungle of life. Since utility will never demand that a thing's causal conditions be made to "disappear" (Valéry) or "stay hidden" (Balzac), the intrinsic connection is as follows: *To possess elegant things and to be elegant by means of them is luxury a priori.* Since luxury is not therefore the same as elegance, and being luxurious does not automatically qualify as elegance, we are dealing with a kind of inverse relationship.

Adorno's phrase "slavery of purposes" is significant as a *genitivus subiectivus*. That is, the purpose of an object defines that object like an authoritarian subject; the purpose is fixed in the appearance, materials and construction of the thing. People in sympathy with totalitarian thinking cynically whitewash the *slavery of purposes* by calling it *form follows function*. But the claim we might therefore want to make, that luxury is the opposite of any demand for functionality, is inexact, for it is only partially correct. There are two possibilities for understanding the opposite of *slavery of purposes*: One, by thinking of the opposite of *slavery*, and the other by thinking of the opposite of *purposes*. In the first case, one thinks of luxury and a liberation from a technocratic utility. The second case is more complicated but builds the bridge to elegance.

From a temporal standpoint, the opposite of determination by purpose is not liberation from this purpose, but determination of some other kind, namely through the temporal opposite of purposes: Through causes. In the first case, in determination by purposes, something is fixed by something in the future. In the second case, in determination through causes, something is fixed by something in the past. Causes necessarily precede effects in time. If something is determined only by causes, it is only determined by the past; it then fulfills no purpose. But if something is determined by a purpose, someone is taking the thought of a thing's use in the future as a reason to make this thing in such a way that it will be able to serve that purpose at some point. Or as Kant says: "The representation of the effect is here the determining ground of its cause and precedes the latter."[28] It means that the future purpose of a thing, mediated through a person acting intentionally, becomes the cause and

Why luxury? **145**

produces causal effects. In this way, something in the future—if actively mediated by a person—determines the appearance, workmanship and construction of a thing.

So, on the one hand, the opposite of Adorno's *slavery of purposes* is certainly luxury understood as emancipation from the domination of purposes. But, on the other hand, we need to recognize the *slavery of causes* as another possible opposite to *slavery of purposes*. Specifically, that means that the opposite of a practical, useful thing is not only an impractical and perhaps luxurious object, but also a thing that was not made for any purpose at all: The purposeless object. Since luxury is the experience of a purpose without purposefulness, luxury can only be experienced with objects that have a purpose and in the use of the thing for this purpose; object without purpose, pure products of causes, are aluxurious *a priori*. This is especially true for nature, at least if that is understood to be exclusively causally determined and purposeless. And yet—and this is the critical difference between luxury and elegance—it may not be possible for nature to be luxurious, but it most certainly can be elegant. A leopard's movement is elegant because for someone observing aesthetically it appears to be—as Valéry described it so well—"carrying without seeming to feel the weight." The animal walks as if free of the laws of physics. In short, the intrinsic relationship between luxury and elegance is this: Elegance is an inverse form of luxury, because elegance is not emancipation from the slavery of purposes as luxury is, but rather emancipation from the slavery of causality. This is, in fact, a form of control and determination of the appearance of things as well, but in a specific, namely a temporal, respect, one of an exactly reversed sort. Briefly stated: In their physical formation, luxuries are and appear to be free from control by the future, while things that are elegant have the effect of having been made free from a past in the physical world.

## Investigation of the question of whether in a judgment of taste the feeling of luxury precedes the judging of the object or the latter precedes the former

One of the most noteworthy questions in the history of aesthetics can be found in §9 of Kant's *Critique of Judgment*—and this, strangely, as the heading of this famous paragraph as well, which Kant himself

**146** The Dadaism of possession

considered to be the most important part in the writing. This heading goes: "Investigation of the question of whether in a judgment of taste the feeling of pleasure precedes the judging of the object or the latter precedes the former."[29] Kant's answer may be surprising at first glance, if we suppose the situation to be clear—first comes the experience of the beautiful, one looks at the thing, finds it beautiful and, on the basis of having had this experience, estimates the observed thing to be beautiful, that is, the decision comes temporally later. But Kant's answer is just the reverse! And with this he discovers an essential feature of aesthetic experience: Aesthetic experiences follow temporally after estimations. That is because aesthetic experiences are reactions of feeling caused by estimations. This fundamentally distinguishes aesthetic experiences from sensual enjoyment, when someone finds something nice or pleasant. Aesthetic experiences are—as the term literally says—experiences in which the aesthetic is inherent. But the concept of the aesthetic refers to a theoretical engagement with themes like perception, beauty and art; when a person is thinking about the aesthetic he is pursuing aesthetics. One can also say that the aesthetic experience is the result of the pursuit of the aesthetic. To put it another way, someone who is not reflecting theoretically and thinking about something aesthetic is not having an aesthetic experience, that is, he has not put himself in a state that would permit him to call something *beautiful*. Aesthetic experience is, then, an experience constituted through theoretical consideration—and this applies to beauty as well as to luxury.

Specifically, it looks like this. If something is experienced as beautiful, then the sense of this object will have previously been considered and found, curiously, to be purposeful, yet without having a purpose. We are dealing with a specific object whose purposefulness does keep making us think about the sense and meaning of the thing, but which also renders the search for a general meaning futile, just because it has no specific purpose. In this way, the one deciding finds himself, according to Kant, in what has become a famous "state of mind involved in the free play of imagination and understanding."[30] This exceptional mental state is self-referential, because a subject becomes aware of his own capacities in this way—which furthermore are capacities that can be attributed to any subject. When something is designated beautiful, it is the result of a projection of a sense of the thing

Why luxury? **147**

on to the thing. The act of consideration produces a specific sensibility in the receiver, which is the reason the receiver calls the thing *beautiful*. Someone who wanted to make fun of Kant might say: With respect to beautiful things, the observer arrogantly pleases himself. The aesthetician Robert Zimmermann—hardly read at all today, and nevertheless among the most important thinkers who anticipated formal aesthetics—pinpoints this peculiarity in his concise language, "the subject enjoys himself in himself [...] one could call this aesthetic self-worship" (tr.).[31]

Whatever one may think of Kant's transcendental argumentation, this is about a structural argument. It looks as though Kant was drawing a blueprint for a description of the reception of luxury. The situation is strikingly analogous, in any case, because what was said of beauty also applies to luxury: An object is not a luxury because someone finds possessing it appealing or stimulating; luxury is nothing appealing. Rather luxury, too, is based on an experience that is structured in a way that is very different from the perception of something as pleasant or comfortable. Whether something is luxurious depends on a kind of self-conscious exchange with the possession, and not with possession alone, as is the case with comfort. Owning something is, in fact, necessary for something to be experienced as luxury, but in itself it is insufficient to constitute the experience: Possession alone is not enough to have a luxury. As with the beautiful, with luxury we are concerned with experiences that differ from the appealing and pleasant in being preceded by a theoretical consideration. That is not the case for pleasant and comfortable things; to produce the appropriate feeling, it is enough for the thing to be consumed and possessed. So comfort and ease can be bought—but not beauty and not luxury either! To put it another way: To find something pleasant, there is no need to have thought about it beforehand. The pleasant, one might say, is related to the beautiful as the comfortable is to luxury; and the beautiful is related in turn to the act of perception as luxury is to the act of possessing, because for the aesthetic experience of luxury the possessor, in order to constitute the experience, must already have come to a decision about his possession. This is the reason the experience of luxury, as well as that of beauty, requires that the possessor have the power of self-conscious judgment. This is because neither beauty nor luxury has a simple sensual effect. For the experience of

**148** The Dadaism of possession

luxury, too, the recipient must reflect on the meaning of the thing, not in the same way he would with the beautiful, but likewise in advance. He must previously have considered whether such a tremendous effort is meaningful, or whether it exceeds both what is technically necessary for something as well as what is anthropologically necessary for someone. This estimation, which is based on a self-conscious power to judge something to be superfluous, irrational and exaggerated, then becomes the condition, in the case of possession—not mere observation—for a genuine form of aesthetic experience, exactly because this experience is felt in reaction to a reflection on this possession.

The statement is ambiguous: *Someone who wants to experience luxury must first consider and decide for himself that something is luxury.* It can, unfortunately, be misunderstood as someone trying to say: *The aesthetic experience of luxury is the product of a linguistic designation of this something as luxury.* If that was what was meant, the interpretationism that was rejected earlier would be back on board, so to speak. That thesis states: Something is luxury because is it interpreted as luxury. But that is exactly what is not the case. It is specifically about the Kantian idea that there are interpretive estimations, made using a power of reflective judgment, that produce a felt reaction and so make an aesthetic experience possible. This aesthetic experience is a felt reaction to a previous decision. It is like this both for beauty and for luxury, if in a different way in each case. For beauty, the aesthetic experience is the effect of a suspended implementation of a search for meaning with no result. The impossibility of access is the sign, the pleasurable attempt to solve a puzzle that cannot be solved in principle. With luxury, the aesthetic experience is the effect of a reflection on transgression as transgression. One reflects on such questions as: Does anyone really need it? Isn't it exaggerated? Is it necessary? Is it appropriate? Is it not unreasonable and irrational? Why should anyone make such a thing so complicated? What is the meaning of so much effort? Specifically, it means that one must *first* reach the decision that a meaningless effort was made, in order to feel, *afterwards*, through one's own possession as a subject putting himself beyond a rational dictum of optimal utility—that is the principle of luxury: The possession of something made for a purpose, but useless or impractical because of the exaggerated effort it requires, permits a subject to experience, as a result of his own judgment, what it is like to voluntarily resist pressure for rational utility, not to meet the usual expectations, not to submit to subtle pressure to find the best solution, not to contribute to greater efficiency under pressure of rationalization—exactly what Max Weber called the rejection of the utilitarian orientation toward use by means of luxury. That is, in using a luxury good he possesses, a person experiences a *purpose without purposefulness* in a particular way: He experiences a specific object as objectively useless or impractical, yet in reflecting on it, experiences it subjectively as useful in order to have the aesthetic self-experience of an autonomous being.

## The conditions of possibility for an experience of luxury: connoisseurship

Another indication that linguistic *estimation as luxury* precedes the subjective *experience of luxury* is that the aesthetic experience of luxury is bound up with the recipient's specialized knowledge and connoisseurship. The reason for this is clear and actually has already been named: In order to be able to experience something as luxury, this something has to have previously been estimated and evaluated with respect to the effort required to make it. But, in order to be able to do that, a certain familiarity with the subject is necessary as a matter of principle, as well as specific information about how the object in question was made; knowledge is needed about the details of the construction, production and history of this object. In this respect, there is no longer any analogy at all to beauty. Rather, another analogy to an estimation of health is given. The question of whether something is healthy or not must be answered, like the question of whether something is luxury, by a specialist. Someone with no knowledge at all can decide whether something is pleasant or comfortable simply by trying it. A person knows whether a chocolate tastes good by eating it. The chocolate does not become a luxury good through its exquisite taste, however, but through a consideration, made prior to eating it, about the enormous effort it took to produce it, and whether such an effort is not simply unreasonable, wasteful and inappropriate for such a brief pleasure. It is clear, the sensuous taste of the chocolate makes no difference whatsoever to the experience of luxury; a luxurious sweet could taste terrible, for there is only an empirical connection between the pleasant, the comfortable

**150** The Dadaism of possession

and the luxurious. Of course, it would be unusual for someone to take a great deal of trouble over the production of a chocolate if it didn't at least taste good. The experience of luxury does require that it be eaten, because only in this way can one know that someone has made an unreasonable effort for this silly purpose.

Someone unfamiliar with a tourbillon will not be able to decide whether such a thing is either exaggerated or appropriate. If he possesses a watch with this elaborate construction he might find it beautiful, or he could wear it as a status symbol, but he would not be able to estimate the effort it represents. For this reason, he cannot possess the watch as a realized refutation of ideals of economy and efficiency, and so cannot experience it as such. Such objective conditions for the estimation of effort can certainly be met in diverse ways. They extend from simple instruction given to the possessor by someone knowledgeable, to a personal competency to estimate. However it may have been acquired, that makes the possessor a connoisseur. Sometimes a little simple information is enough to recognize exaggerated effort, for example, to learn that the ingredients of a menu have been flown in from all over the world, or that an automobile has been built by hand. But in either case, the special knowledge puts a person in a position to be able to recognize that something involves effort that is technically not necessary. Now that is not to say that the recognition of something as luxury is the same thing as the specialist recognition of the effort. An object of exaggerated complexity can be a luxury good, but isn't one *per se*. The concern is, rather, with the description of dependencies, and the remarkable thing is that in the case of the experience of luxury's dependence on the estimation of effort, there are two *a priori* dependencies at play. For one thing, in the metaphorical sense of *a priori*, the informed estimation of effort is logically necessary for the experience of luxury; for another, however, in the literal sense of *a priori*, the estimation must come temporally before the experience. A judgment of luxury, such as *this watch is a luxury*, is not only a linguistic interpretation of this watch as luxury; the judgment of luxury with respect to the watch also projects onto the watch an experience of the watch which could only have arisen in the subject on the basis of the necessary and prior estimation of the watch as something of exaggerated complexity, and of the possessor's possession of the watch.

Why luxury? **151**

## Aesthetes *versus* enthusiasts

As comparable as the experiences of beauty and of luxury are with respect to their common reliance on a prior decision, they have equally significant differences in the attitudes from which these decisions are respectively made. The contrast between the prototypical positions of aesthetes and enthusiasts offers a way to describe this difference. An enthusiast is someone who is interested in all experiences of luxury; an aesthete, however, is someone in search of the experience of beauty in as many aspects of life as possible. Seen in this way, we are dealing with different interests that share an underlying view. Both aesthetes and enthusiasts are convinced that a successful life requires us to free ourselves from the domination of utilitarian reason alone. That is, efficient expedience is as much the enemy as either *purposefulness without purpose* or *purpose without purposefulness*. But, in spite of this common ground, enthusiasts and aesthetes approach these things from two genuinely opposing attitudes. The aesthete can realize his interest in the beauty of things as long as he remains completely indifferent and unconcerned with respect to the way the things are made. It is entirely different for the enthusiast, who must know the thing thoroughly and be interested in it. This difference in attitude can, in an extreme case, lead to a real confrontation between two conflicting lifestyles. If luxury's form of reception is important to someone's life, he will find a contemplative aesthete irritating. For the latter, in his life, cultivates exactly those things the former perceives to be superficial naïveté, and which from his standpoint are veiled as bourgeois disinterest. Because, for the enthusiast, the disinterested attitude Kant described is bound up with a questionable point of view, namely one with a tendency toward superficiality, that is, an aestheticism. And this objection is not to be brushed off lightly.

In the *Critique of Judgment*, Kant mentions a palace that could only be considered beautiful by someone who, in his disinterest, deliberately disregarded the fact that this palace had been built under inhuman conditions. This can be made more exact and specific: In the discussion of disinterest, Kant describes an approach to aesthetic reception in which a carpet knotted by the bloody hands of children under miserable conditions could actually be found beautiful. Another example, perhaps less drastic but far more widespread, would be a

**152** The Dadaism of possession

well-heeled theatergoer who watches the work of actors who are on stage for a pittance, with no benefits, in contemplative disinterest, even though it would be nothing for him to pay twice as much for a ticket. In both cases, the special aesthetic experience of beauty can arise only because the observer must—as Kant emphasizes many times—"preserve complete indifference"[32] toward the conditions of production. The receiver positions himself so as to be "indifferent as to the existence of an object."[33] Very accurately, and in the spirit of any enthusiast, Adorno calls this attitude toward reception "cold-hearted contemplation"[34] for exactly this reason.

It is the aesthetic attitude in the estimation of the beautiful that has such diverse effects on outsiders. On the one hand, it often has a refreshingly masterful effect, exactly with respect to the enthusiasts' know-it-all detail that a connoisseur occasionally displays. Someone may be thoroughly unimpressed with the great technical effort involved in some thing and come straight to an aesthetic judgment: *But it is still plug-ugly.* On the other hand, it is not rare for contemplation to have the effect of being a refuge for naïveté, philistinism and ignorance. It must even be said that someone interested only in the beauty of things runs the risk of contemplatively overlooking the conditions of production even when this is inappropriate. It is odd, in fact completely incomprehensible, that Kant does not devote a single word to the dangers of aestheticism, although he sketches the worldview in detail. In the *Critique of Judgment*, not one sentence examines the question of what criterion would make it possible to decide when an attitude of disinterest may be taken. When may we contemplate? When may we be coldhearted? These are by no means unimportant questions, for there are plenty of situations in which it would simply be cynical and decadent to behave contemplatively—for example, just to take pleasure in the beauty of the bloodstained carpet. But these questions do not even present themselves to an enthusiast. For to consider something a luxury one cannot behave with contemplative indifference toward the existence of the thing and the conditions under which it came to be.

Someone who wants to experience luxury must consider something to be luxury, which, however, is impossible "as long as it confines itself to self-satisfied contemplation."[35] Rather, the thing must be critically considered, for a determination must be made about whether an

Why luxury? **153**

irrational effort has been or will be made. Because someone in search of an experience of luxury must become the possessor of the thing; but as possessor, he is necessarily interested in the thing and must—in contrast to the aesthete—take responsibility for its existence. This is the reason the experience of luxury rests on an aesthetic attitude that perhaps does not, in comparison to the aesthetic attitude toward the experience of beauty, necessarily demand a different approach to morality, but certainly suggests one and creates sensitivity to it. To speak as Adorno: Someone who is not contemplative is not yet warm-hearted on those grounds, but at least he is no longer coldhearted. Someone who, in his irrationalism, treasures a carpet for its millions of knots, is interested in the question of who tied these knots, how the carpet became possible. The enthusiast does not dismiss such questions. Rather, they form the basis for the possibility of speaking of an exaggerated complexity. But in this way it is also always possible to take the view that this is *no longer* a thing that merely exceeds in effort what is necessary for humans, but a thing whose fabrication disregards human rights—that is something different and morally reprehensible. So someone who is willing to cross the boundaries of appropriateness with his possessions, but not to break moral laws, must know what he owns. This is not to say that there are no enthusiasts who cynically accustom themselves to the fact that children knotted the carpet. That can never be ruled out. But it should not make us lose sight of having two different aesthetic attitudes under consideration, which make two different aesthetic experiences possible and that imply two different moral tendencies. The aesthete could inquire about the conditions of the carpet's manufacture when he is buying it—not all aesthetes are cynics!—but he does not have to, because for his aesthetic experience this information is completely irrelevant and potentially disruptive; he really should not be interested in the existence or the production of the thing at all.

Imagine two watches, an original and a copy. It is impossible to tell them apart from the outside, even looking through a magnifying glass no difference can be detected. But there is a difference: There is an extremely complex tourbillon ticking in the one, and a dime-a-dozen clockwork in the other. The externally invisible difference between these watches may not and cannot play any role in the aesthetic experience of their beauty, for a complicated production does not

**154** The Dadaism of possession

make something more beautiful or less beautiful. The one watch may be a work of art, the other not, the one watch may be important from the standpoint of cultural history, the other not, the one watch may be valuable, the other not, but both—the original and the forgery—are equally beautiful, because knowing the difference is unimportant for the estimation of beauty. We see once again how luxury is different—in this respect, luxury is once again the opposite of beauty: The aesthetic experience here depends on the possessor's knowledge. While authenticity may be irrelevant to an aesthete as long as the beauty is there, an enthusiast cannot easily tolerate forgeries. For as soon as a connoisseur discovers that he has mistaken a simple watch for a complex masterpiece, the possibility of further experiencing this watch as a transgression of the usual notions of appropriate effort is abruptly at an end.

This shows that the enthusiast's need to be knowledgeable about effort has an almost inevitable effect on his lifestyle. In order to be able to value and make decisions concerning the effort associated with something accurately, he must himself make an effort with his own affairs, so to speak, which is not rarely comparable in its irrationality and effort to a luxury good. To become and to remain a connoisseur takes effort. It is time-consuming and strenuous. One may try to avoid the effort of being knowledgeable by just relying on available information without having one's own specialist knowledge. So, by putting one's trust in a dealer, one can learn that a tourbillon is a complicated and capricious construction that offers hardly any advantage in terms of the watch's precision. Such secondhand knowledge, memorized without understanding, can in fact be used to make estimates, but in a way that does not then rest on personal knowledge and that carries the danger of being feigned knowledge. But, since we are not concerned with correct linguistic interpretations in connection with luxury, that is, not with the correct way of speaking about the issue, but rather about the private experience, in fact about breaking with one's own ideas about appropriate effort, one may doubt whether appropriated external information allows for the experience in the same way as would an insight into a realized irrationality that rests on one's own specialist knowledge. Because the corresponding statement would then actually have to be: *Others say to me that this thing before me represents a ludicrous, utterly impractical and unjustifiable effort; I cannot explain why this is so, however. Others say to me that I could experience luxury here.* To be sure that this will not happen, one particular path is particularly reliable: Do it yourself, and here the difference between the enthusiasts and the aesthetes reappears.

## Do it yourself

In a legal context, just four kinds of possession normally come into play: Buying, stealing, inheriting and receiving as a gift. But there is at least one more, a fifth way to take possession of something, which is particularly significant in connection with the experience of luxury: Making it yourself. With respect to the knowledge of a given effort, making it yourself is the exact opposite of information acquired secondhand. Someone who has planted and cared for an orchid garden himself, for example, no longer needs to be told how much effort was needed. Doing something unnecessary yourself provides an authentic perspective on exaggerated effort, which is the basis for an experience of luxury. Once again, the difference between beauty and luxury is in evidence, because aesthetes usually have little more than contempt for doing it yourself—at least from their point of view whether one made it oneself or paid a high price for it makes no difference to the thing's beauty. Aesthetes distinguish rigorously between genesis and value. Enthusiasts, by contrast, approach self-fabrication with the greatest respect; for them it is the incontestable grounds and the incontrovertible evidence for knowledge of the thing. Making something oneself is to some extent the purest expression of that which interests those concerned with questions of production—which is the very thing that is, in turn, the condition for the desired experience of luxury. Furthermore, possession represents real control over something, after all, which can be exercised in very different ways. The experience of luxury's connection to the actual implementation of the desire to possess suggests that there is a proportional relationship between the strength of the desire to possess and the way the experience of luxury manifests itself. Someone who simply buys a luxury good does not necessarily become the possessor by doing so, which he must be, however, in order to be able to have the experience of luxury. The buyer of something may have merely acquired some property. The same holds for filching, inheriting and receiving things as gifts. Only making

**156** The Dadaism of possession

something oneself is fundamentally different, which is why making things oneself has an intrinsic relationship to the experience of luxury. Someone who makes or restores something himself necessarily possesses and knows it simultaneously. Making something with irrational effort is inevitably bound up with both the experience of what it is like to have a possession that took enormous effort to make, and with the capacity to explain and recognize this exaggerated effort—and this very combination of possession and connoisseurship is the basis for all the experiences of luxury that occur, not infrequently, in connection with old, obsolete devices.

One quite often hears it said that things once considered luxuries now qualify as normal, everyday objects. In the 1950s, for example, possession of a simple automobile would have been a luxury for most people. But the problem with this view is that luxury is being identified, if not actually confused, with comfort. What one is actually trying to say is that many technologies have turned what was once a rare level of comfort into a common one. But being a luxury is not necessarily connected with either rarity or comfort. Rather, it is connected with an exaggerated and irrational effort. We must therefore go on to confirm that in contrast to the usual, widespread view, the exact opposite is the case for luxury. It is normally not the case that luxury goods become common, but rather that perfectly common things become elaborate through technical development, so that their continued use therefore opens opportunities for luxury. Many things that were not considered in connection with luxury because of their simplicity become, of their own accord, objects that are possessed and cared for specifically for this experience. Technically efficient, modest and economical things—such as, say, the compact cars of the 1950s—over the years become things whose continued use requires that their possessors be familiar with them, or at least expend exceptional effort. Practical things become impractical things, and so candidates for experiences of luxury. It is easy to find many further examples. Although nothing has changed in the technology of vinyl records itself, in light of newer, more efficient possibilities, keeping and caring for this technology no longer seems practical. The same thing applies to the use of a normal, everyday camera from the 1970s. In fact, someone who wants to continue to photograph using film must go to an irrational amount of trouble that can no longer be justified on utilitarian grounds.

## The existence of luxury: indicators instead of proofs

A conclusion can now be reached, because the difference has become clear. Estimations of the beautiful and of the luxurious are made from two diametrically opposed attitudes with respect to the aesthetic object. A disinterested consideration of what is perceived is the condition for the experience of the beautiful, just as a consideration of the use of a possession with specialist knowledge is the condition for the experience of luxury. But as different as these two conditions are, they share the same problem. It is, and remains, unclear how we can be sure that something is valued *for an aesthetic experience*. Here, once again, Kant is silent. He neither names a criterion for *when* a contemplative attitude of disinterest with respect to something would be opportune, nor does he devote a single word to how we can be sure *whether* someone really has taken such an attitude. He describes disinterest as the necessary condition of possibility for a judgment of taste *en détail*, but formulates no criterion with which to determine whether someone fulfills this criterion, that is, whether someone is actually making a disinterested estimate of something. Perhaps someone is just trying it on, pretending to be disinterested. This absence of a criterion is a serious problem that arises for the aesthetic experience of luxury as well, and leaves it wide open to suppositions. The analogy can be pinpointed with two questions. For one, how can we decide whether someone is observing something impartially, for the sake of an experience of beauty? For another, how can we decide whether someone possesses a thing on the basis of specialist knowledge, for the sake of an aesthetic experience of luxury? The answer is identical in both cases—we can't! There is no proof, because neither is recognizable to an outsider. The appearance of disinterest can deceive, as can a feigned refusal of instrumental rationality on the basis of specialist knowledge.

We can even go one step further and claim that the recipient himself may not be in a position to know whether he is, respectively, observing something disinterestedly or possessing something on the basis of connoisseurship. That would then mean that someone who falsely believed himself to be viewing or possessing something for the sake of an aesthetic experience was really doing it for the sake of social prestige and repressing this reason, not wanting it to be the

**158** The Dadaism of possession

case. So, a reader of novels may in fact set out to consider the works in a disinterested way, but *really* just chases after the canon of the academic educational elite for the sake of social recognition. These views that take such self-deception for possible become thinkable, at least, when the unconscious is assumed to be part of the argument. That which applies to the beautiful then also applies to those luxury goods a person treasures. The splendid garden with exotic plants may, in fact, be an especially elaborate one, owned and cared for by a connoisseur, but—and such an objection is always possible—*really* he is only displaying his financial options here. From the outside, no one can recognize whether beautiful and luxurious things are cherished for the sake of private aesthetic experience or as a social status symbol. The annoying result is that anyone who sets out to gain aesthetic experience can be accused of just being ostentatious and affected—without being able to defend himself. That is to some extent the common fate of luxury and beauty, if both phenomena are thought to be forms of aesthetic experience. There is no proof whether and when someone is really having such an exceptional experience, to say nothing of whether this experience really does, like an anthropologically pregnant moment, provide a sense of one's own life. Skeptics—but also malicious people—can always object that *purpose without purposefulness* or *purposefulness without purpose* in fact fulfill hidden interests and so are useful. In the end, therefore, each of us is inevitably alone with the experience of beauty and of luxury. Because no one doubts the existence of either the naïve use of aesthetic objects as ostentation or on the no less naïve homage to the middle-class canon of beauty. But just because such *self-presentation by means of aesthetic objects* exists does not mean that they are all that exists, and it especially does not mean that there can be no *experience of self by means of aesthetic objects*—even if the only available indicator of its existence is a personal report of experience or a phenomenological description. That is certainly not a lot, but it is also not nothing, and above all, a phenomenology of luxury is not concerned with proving to someone that something or other in the world is luxury; it is not about proof at all, but solely about indicators of phenomena that each of us must finally experience for ourselves to be persuaded of their reality. The guiding hope is that through description we will become more sensitive to it and will notice the phenomenon—should it appear.

Why luxury? **159**

# Notes

1 Theodor W. Adorno, "Veblen's Attack on Culture" in *Prisms*, trans. Samuel Weber and Shierry Weber (Cambridge: MIT Press, 1981 [1941]), 73.
2 Theodor W. Adorno, *Minima Moralia: Reflections from a Damaged Life*, trans. E.F.N. Jephcott (London: Verso, 2005 [1951]), § 50, 91.
3 Theodor W. Adorno, "Minima Moralia. Reflexionen aus dem beschädigten Leben," in Theodor W. Adorno, ed., *Gesammelte Schriften*, Vol. 4 (Frankfurt/M.: 2003 [1951]). Appendix, 91. Appendix was not included in the English translation.
4 Bazon Brock, "Luxurieren als soziale Strategie," in *Georg Hornemann: Objets d'art, Ring zur Skulptur*, Austellungskatalog (Duisburg: Lehmbruck-Museum, 2012), 15–23.
5 Theodor W. Adorno, "Veblen's Attack on Culture in *Prisms*, trans. Samuel Weber and Shierry Weber (Cambridge: MIT Press, 1981 [1941]), 80.
6 Theodor W. Adorno, *Aesthetic Theory*, trans. Robert Hullot-Kentor (London and New York: Continuum, 2002 [1970]), 1.
7 ibid., 5.
8 Adorno, "Veblen's Attack," 86.
9 ibid.
10 Adorno, *Aesthetic Theory*, 37.
11 ibid., 227.
12 ibid.
13 Adorno, "Veblen's Attack," 86.
14 ibid.
15 Adorno, *Aesthetic Theory*, 133.
16 ibid., 4.
17 ibid.,138.
18 Adorno, "Veblens Attack," 75.
19 Adorno, *Aesthetic Theory*, 1.
20 ibid., 13.
21 ibid., 12.
22 ibid., 225.
23 ibid., 5.
24 ibid., 227.
25 Heinrich von Kleist, *Über das Marionettentheater* (Stuttgart: Reclam, 2013) 13.
26 Honoré de Balzac, "Abhandlung über das elegante Leben," in Edgar Pankow, ed. and translator *Pathologie des Soziallebens* (Leipzig: Reclam, 2002 [1830]), 74.
27 Paul Valéry, *Cahiers*, vol. 1, trans. Paul Gifforf, Siân Miles, Robert Pickering and Brian Stimpson (Frankfurt/M.: Peter Lang, 2000 [1973]), 278.
28 Immanuel Kant, *Critique of Judgement*, trans. James Creed Meredith, revised by Nicolas Walker (Oxford: Oxford University Press, 2007), §10, 51.
29 ibid., §9, 48.
30 ibid., §9, 49.
31 Robert Zimmermann, "Zur Reform der Aesthetik als exacter Wissenschaft," in 315 in *Zeitschrift für exakte Philosophie*, 2 (1862).

**160** The Dadaism of possession

32 Kant, *Critique of Judgment*, §2, p. 37.
33 ibid., §5, 41.
34 Adorno, *Minima Moralia*, §149, 235.
35 Theodor W. Adorno, "Cultural Criticism and Society," in Theodor W. Adorno, ed., *Prisms*, trans. Samuel Weber and Shierry Weber (Cambridge: MIT Press, 1981 [1949]), 34.

# DETAILED TABLE OF CONTENTS

*Foreword*                                                                                          *vi*

Introduction                                                                                          1

**PART I**
**Play, then war, anxiety and drugs—and now: luxury       11**

1    Anthropology and the idea of self-experience 13
     The idea of a substitution 13 – The whole human being 14 – The
     whole human being conceived a balanced human being 15 – The
     whole human being conceived as a human being with self- experi-
     ence 16 – The effect of playing: an experience of self 18 – Friedrich
     Schiller's 14th letter 21 – The challenge of seeing for oneself 22 -
     Under anaesthesia 24 – The pregnant moment 25 – The pregnant
     moment in anthropology 27 – The problem of the structural
     whole 29

2    Aesthetics and the search for moments of self-experience 33
     Friedrich Schiller's suggestion: grasp being in its entirety 33 –
     Why play, actually? 34 – Martin Heidegger: anxiety instead of
     play 36 – Ernst Jünger: adventure instead of play 40 – The many
     pregnant moments 42 – An example from art history: the double
     pregnant moment 43 – The search for the pregnant moment 46

**162** Detailed table of contents

## PART II
## Luxury: the Dadaism of Possession 51

3   The judgment of luxury 53
    The matters at issue and the sense of the concept 53 – The standard
    definition 57 – Luxury *versus* comfort 58 – Luxury *versus* ostentation
    61 – Necessary for something and necessary for someone 65 – A form
    of life at the middle level 66 – The two levels of the judgment of
    luxury 69 – The judgment of luxury's claim to generality 71 –
    Luxury and the concept of the healthy 74 – Luxury judgment and
    evaluations 76 – Luxury: a product of interpretation? 77 – The limits
    of interpretationism 79 – Having an illness and having luxury 82

4   Luxury: a special aesthetic experience 85
    When is Luxury? 85 – Features of aesthetic experience I:
    an operational orientation 87 – Features of aesthetic experience II:
    self-referentiality 89 – Luxury: a special aesthetic experience 90 –
    Ownership *versus* possession 93 – Luxury: operationally oriented pos-
    session 95 – Luxury's self-referentiality 100 – Intellectuals' resentment
    of an aesthetic of possession 102 – Luxury: a defiant *Lebensgefühl* 107 –
    The Dadaism of possession 111 – What is open to criticism about
    luxury? 116 – Without purpose: nonpurposeful and unpurposeful
    117 – Two forms of transgression: inadequacy and excess 120 –
    Luxury and rarity 123 – Why luxury? Social pressure 125

5   Why Luxury? 132
    Why luxury? The longing for freedom 132 – Luxury and art 134 –
    Art: luxury without purpose 137 – Luxury and elegance 140 –
    Investigation of the question of whether in a judgment of luxury the
    experience of luxury precedes the judging of the object or the latter
    precedes the former 145 – The conditions of possibility for an
    experience of luxury: connoisseurship 149 – Aesthetes *versus* enthusi-
    asts 151 – Do it yourself 155 – The existence of luxury: indicators
    instead of proofs 157

*Detailed table of contents*                                          *161*
*Bibliography*                                                         *163*
*Index*                                                               *169*

# BIBLIOGRAPHY

Adorno, Theodor, *Philosophische Terminologie*, edited by Rudolf zur Lippe. Frankfurt/M.: Suhrkamp, 1973.

Adorno, Theodor W., "Veblen's Attack on Culture" 73–94 and "Cultural Criticism and Society" 17-34 in Theodor W. Adorno, ed. *Prisms*, translated by Samuel Weber and Shierry Weber. Cambridge: MIT Press, 1981 [1941].

Adorno, Theodor W., *Aesthetic Theory*, translated by Robert Hullot-Kentor. London and New York: Continuum, 2002 [1970].

Adorno, Theodor W., "Minima Moralia. Reflexionen aus dem beschädigten Leben" in Theodor W. Adorno, ed. *Gesammelte Schriften*, vol . 4. Frankfurt/M.: 2003 [1951], Appendix, 91. Appendix was not included in the English translation.

Adorno, Theodor W., *Minima Moralia: Reflections from a Damaged Life*, translated by E.F.N. Jephcott. London: Verso, 2005 [1951], § 50, 91.

Adorno, Theodor W., *Theorie der Halbbildung* [Theory of Half Education]. Frankfurt/M.: Suhrkamp, 2006 [1959].

Balzac, Honoréde, "Abhandlung über das elegante Leben" [Treatise on the Elegant Life] 38–97 in Edgar Pankow, ed., *Pathologie des Soziallebens*. Leipzig: Reclam, 2002 [1830].

Baudrillart, Henri Joseph Léon, *Histoire du luxe privé et public, depuis l'antiquité jusqu'à nos jours*. Paris: Hachette, 1878.

Benjamin, Walter, "Unpacking my Library: A Talk about Book Collecting" 59–67 in Hannah Arendt, ed. *Illuminations*, translated by Harry Zohn. New York: Schocken, 1969 [1931].

Berg, Maxine and Elizabeth Eger, eds. *Luxury in the Eighteenth Century: Debates and Delectable Goods*. London: Palgrave, 2003.

Berry, Christopher J., *The Idea of Luxury: A Conceptual and Historical Investigation*. Cambridge: Cambridge University Press, 1994.

**164** Bibliography

Bourdieu, Pierre, *Distinction: A Social Critique of the Judgment of Taste*, translated by Richard Nice. Cambridge: Harvard University Press, 1984 [1979].

Brock, Bazon, "Luxurieren als soziale Strategie" 15–23 in *Georg Hornemann: Objets d'art, Ring zur Skulptur*, exhibition catalogue. Duisburg: Lehmbruck-Museum, 2012.

Enzensberger, Hans, Magnus, "Luxus: woher, und wohin damit? Reminiszenzen an den Überfluß" [Luxury: Where Does it Come From and Where Is it Going? Reminiscences on Abundance] 143–161 in Hans Magnus Enzensberger, ed. *Zickzack, Aufsätze*. Frankfurt/M.: Suhrkamp, 1997 [1995].

Fromm, Erich, *To Have or to Be*. London and New York: Continuum, 1997 [1976].

Gehlen, Arnold, "Luxus und Gesellschaft," [Luxury and Society] 529–541 in Karl-Siegbert Rehberg, ed. *Die Seele im technischen Zeitalter und andere soziologische Schriften und Kulturanalysen* [The Soul in the Age of Technology and other Sociological Writings and Cultural Analyses]. Frankfurt/M.: Vittorio Klostermann, 2004 [1968].

Geiger, Moritz, *Zugänge zur Ästhetik* [Approaches to Aesthetics]. Leipzig: Der neue Geist, 1928.

Görland, Albert, "Über den Begriff des Luxus: Eine philosophische Kritik" [On the Concept of Luxury. A Philosophical Critique] 27–45 in *Kant-Studien* 31, 1926.

Gumbrecht, Hans Ulrich, *In Praise of Athletic Beauty*. Cambridge and London: Harvard University Press, 2006.

Hegel, Georg, Wilhelm, Friedrich, *Aesthetics: Lectures on Fine Art*, Vol. II, translated by John Knox. Oxford: Clarendon Press, 1975 [1820–1829].

Hegel, Georg,Wilhelm, Friedrich, *Philosophie des Rechts: Die Vorlesung von 1819/ 20 in einer Nachschrift*. Frankfurt/M.: Suhrkamp, 1983, [1819–1820], 155.

Hegel, Georg, Wilhelm, Friedrich, *Elements of the Philosophy of Right*, translated by H.B. Nisbet. Cambridge: Cambridge University Press, 1991 [1821].

Heidegger, Martin, "What is Metaphysics?" 353–392 in *Existence and Being*, with introduction by Werner Brock and translated by R. F. C. Hull and Allan Crick. Chicago: Henry Regnery, 1949 [1929].

Heidegger, Martin, *Nietzsche*, Vols. I and II, translated by David Farrell Krell. San Francisco: HarperCollins, 1991 [1936–1939].

Heidegger, Martin, *The Fundamental Concepts of Metaphysics: World, Finitude, Solitude*. Indianapolis: Indiana University Press, 1995 [1929–1930].

Heidegger, Martin, *Being and Time*, translated by John Macquarrie and Edward Robinson. Oxford and Cambridge: Blackwell, 2001 [1927].

Heidegger, Martin, *Übungen für Anfänger. Schillers Briefe über die ästhetische Erziehung des Menschen* [Exercises for Beginners: Schiller's Letters on the Aesthetic Education of Man]. Marbach am Neckar: Deutsche Schillergeschellschaft, 2005 [1936–1937].

Bibliography **165**

Hume, David, "Of Refinement in the Arts" 167–177 in Stephen Copley and Andrew Edgar, eds. *Selected Essays*. Oxford and New York: Oxford University Press, 1993 [1752].

Husserl, Edmund, *Analyses Concerning Passive and Active Synthesis: Lectures on Transcendental Logic*, translated by Anthony J. Steinbeck. Dordrecht and London: Kluwer Academic Publishers, 2001 [1918–1926].

Jaeggi, Rahel, *Kritik von Lebensformen* [Critique of Forms of Life]. Berlin: Suhrkamp, 2014.

Jaspers, Karl, "Mein Weg zur Philosophie," [My Way to Philosophy] 323–332 in *Rechenschaft und Ausblick: Reden und Aufsätze*. Munich: Piper, 1951.

Jaspers, Karl, *Philosophy, Vol. 2: Existential Elucidation*, translated by E.B. Ashton Chicago and London: The University of Chicago Press, 1970 [1932].

Jung, Matthias, *Gewöhliche Erfahrung* [Everyday Experience]. Tübingen: Mohr Sieback, 2014.

Jünger, Ernst, *Der Kampf als inneres Erlebnis* [Combat as Inner Experience]. Berlin: E.S. Mittler and Son, 1922.

Jünger, Ernst, *Approaches: Drugs and Ecstatic Intoxication*, Internet Archive, https://archive.org/details/ApproachesDrugsAndEcstaticIntoxicationErnst Junger1/page/n7, 1970.

Jünger, Ernst, "Über den Schmerz" [On Pain] 143–191 in *Sämtliche Werke*, Vol. 7. Stuttgart: Klett-Cotta, 1980 [1934].

Jünger, Ernst, *Storm of Steel*, translated by Michael Hofmann. London: Penguin, 2004.

Kant, Immanuel, *Critique of Judgment*, translated by James Creed Meredith, edited by Nicolas Walker. Oxford: Oxford University Press, 2007.

Kleist, Heinrich, von, *Über das Marionettentheater*. Stuttgart: Reclam, 2013 [1810].

Krockow, Christian, Graf von, *Die Heimkehr zum Luxus: Von der Notwendigkeit des Überflussigen* [Luxury Comes Home: On the Necessity of the Superfluous]. Zurich: Kreuz, 1989.

Krünitz, Johann, Georg, *Oeconomische Encyklopädie oder allgemeines System der Land-, Haus- und Staats-Wirtschaft* [Encyclopedia of Economics or General System for Managing Land, Buildings and the State], 1773–1858, Vol. 82. Berlin: Joachim Pauli, 1801.

Laszlo, Carl, *Aufruf zum Luxus und Andere Manifeste* [Call to Luxury and Other Manifestos]. Stuttgart: Collispress Paul Eckhardt, 1960.

Laszlo, Carl, "Bevor Neo-Dada da war, war Dada da" [Before Neo-Dada was there, there was Dada] (1966) in Carl Laszlo, ed. *Aufruf zum Luxus und Andere Manifeste* [Call to Luxury and Other Manifestos]. Stuttgart: Collispress Paul Eckhardt, 1967.

Lessing, Gotthold, Ephraim, *Laocoön: An Essay upon the Limits of Painting and Poetry*, translated by Ellen Frothingham. Boston: Roberts Brothers, 1887 [1766].

**166** Bibliography

Lessing, Gotthold, Ephraim, "Emilia Galotti" 31–103 in *Five German Tragedies*. Harmondsworth: Penguin, 1969 [1772].

Mandeville, Bernard, *The Fable of the Bees, or Private Vices, Publick Benefits*, 3rd edition. London: J. Tonson, 1724 [1714].

Marx, Karl, *Capital: A Critique of Political Economy*, Vol. 1, translated by Samuel Moore and Edward Aveling. Moscow: Progress Publishers, 2015 [1867].

Merleau-Ponty, Maurice, *Phenomenology of Perception*, translated by Colin Smith. London: Routledge, 1962 [1945].

Merleau-Ponty, Maurice, *In Praise of Philosophy*, translated by John Wild and James Edie. Evanston: Northwestern University Press, 1963 [1953].

Meyer, Thorsten and Reinhold Reith, eds. *Luxus und Konsum: Eine historische Annäherung*. Münster: Waxmann, 2003.

Mühlmann, Horst, *Luxus und Komfort: Wortgeschichte und Wortvergleich* [Luxury and Comfort: Word History and Word Comparison]. Bonn: Rheinische Friedrich-Wilhelms Universität, 1975.

Nietzsche, Friedrich, "On the Utility and Liability of History for Life" 83–167 in Giorgio Colli and Mazzino Montinari, eds.*Unfashionable Observations*, Vol. 2, translated by Richard T. Gray. Stanford: Stanford University Press, 1995 [1874].

Pfaller, Robert, *Wofür es sich zu leben lohnt: Elemente materialistischer Philosophie* [Why Living is Worthwhile: Elements of Materialist Philosophy]. Frankfurt/M.: Fischer, 2011.

Pfänders, Alexander, *Phänomenologie des Wollens: eine psychologische Analyse. Motive und Motivationen* [Phenomenology of the Will: A Psychological Analysis. Motives and Motivations]. Munich: Barth, 1963.

Rosa, Hartmut, *Weltbeziehungen im Zeitalter der Beschleunigung, Umrisse einer neuen Gesellschaftskritik* [Global Relationships in the Age of Acceleration: Outline of a New Social Criticism]. Berlin: Suhrkamp, 2012.

Rousseau, Jean-Jacques, *Emile, or on Education*, translated by Allan Bloom. New York: Basic Books, 1979 [1762].

Sartre, Jean-Paul, *Existentialism and Humanism*, translated by Philip Mairet. London: Eyre Methuen, 1973 [1946], 34.

Sartre, Jean-Paul, *Being and Nothingness: An Essay on Phenomenological Ontology*, translated by Hazel E. Barnes. London: Routledge, 2003 [1943].

Sartre, Jean-Paul, *The Imaginary: A Phenomenological Psychology of the Imagination*, translated by Jonathan Webber. London and New York: Routledge, 2004 [1940].

Scheler, Max, "Lehre von den drei Tatsachen" [The Theory of the Three Facts] 431–502 in *Schriften aus dem Nachlass* [Writings from the Estate of Max Scheler], Vol. 1. Bern: Francks Verlag, 1957 [1911/1912].

Schiller, Friedrich, "Brief vom 18.2.1793 an Gottfried Koerner [Letter to Gottfried Koerner on February 18, 1793] 18–24 in *Schillers Briefwechsel mit Körner. Von 1784 bis zum Tode Schillers* [Schiller's Correspondence with

## Bibliography  167

Körner: From 1784 to Schiller's Death] Part 2: 1793–1805. Leipzig: Veit, 1859.

Schiller, Friedrich, *On the Aesthetic Education of Man in a Series of Letters*, edited and translated by Elizabeth M. Wilkinson and L.A. Willoughby. Oxford: Clarendon Press, 2005 [1795].

Schlegel, Friedrich von, "Athenäums Fragmente" [Fragments from the *Athenaeum* Journal] 105–156 in Ernst Behler and Hans Eichner, eds. *Kritische Schriften und Fragmente: Studienausgabe* [Writings and Fragments: Student Edition], Vol. 2. Paderborn: Ferdinand Schöningh, 1988 [1798].

Schwitters, Kurt, "Brief vom 24.7.1946 an Christof Spengemann" [Letter of 24 July 1946 to Christof Spengemann] 208–212 in Ernst Nündel, eds. *Wir Spielen, bis uns der Tod abholt: Briefe aus fünf Jahrzehnten* [We'll Play until Death Gets Us: Letters from Five Decades]. Frankfurt/M., Berlin and Vienna: Ullstein, 1974.

Seel, Martin, "Ästhetik und Aisthetik" [Aesthetic and Aisthetic] 17–38 in Birgit Recki and Lambert Wiesing, eds. *Bild und Reflexion, Paradigmen und Perspektiven der gegenwärtigen Ästhetik* [Image and Reflection, Paradigms and Perspectives in Contemporary Aesthetics]. Munich: Wilhelm Fink, 1997.

Sekora, John, *Luxury: The Concept in Western Thought, Eden to Smollett*. Baltimore and London: Johns Hopkins University Press, 1977.

Sloterdijk, Peter, *Not Saved: Essays after Heidegger*, translated by Ian Alexander Moore and Christopher Turner. Cambridge: Polity Press, 2017 [2001].

Sombart, Werner, *Luxury and Capitalism*, translated by W.R. Dittmar. Ann Arbor: University of Michigan Press, 1967 [1913].

Sommers, Manfred, *Suchen und Finden: lebensweltlich Formen* [Search and Find: Forms in the Life World]. Frankfurt/M.: Suhrkamp, 2002.

Ullrich, Wolfgang, *Habenwollen: Wie funktioniert die Konsumkultur?* [Wanting to Have: How Does Consumer Culture Work?]. Frankfurt/M.: Fischer, 2008 [2006].

Ullrich, Wolfgang, "Besitzen statt rezipieren: Wie die Ikonographie zeitgenössischer Kunstsammler die Ideale moderner Kunst revidiert" [Possessing Instead of Receiving: How Contemporary Art Collectors' Iconography is Revising the Ideals of Modern Art] 121–129 in *Pop. Kultur & Kritik* 5, 2014.

Urwick, Edward Johns, *Luxury and Waste of Life*. London: J.M.Dent, 1908.

Valéry, Paul, *Cahiers* [Notebooks], Vol. 1, translated by Paul Gifforf, Siân Miles, Robert Pickering and Brian Stimpson. Frankfurt/M.: Peter Lang, 2000 [1973].

Veblen, Thorstein, *The Theory of the Leisure Class*. Oxford: Oxford University Press, 2007 [1999].

Verne, Jules, *Around the World in Eighty Days*, translated by George Makepeace Towle. Boston: James Osgood, 1873.

Weber, Max, *Economy and Society: An Outline of Interpretive Sociology*, translated by Guenther Roth and Claus Wittich. Berkeley, Los Angeles and London: University of California Press, 1978 [1921].

## 168 Bibliography

Weder, Christine and Maximilian Bergengruen, eds. *Luxus:Die Ambivalenz des Überflussigen in der Moderne* [Luxury: The Ambivalence of Abundance in Modernity], Göttingen: Wallstein, 2011.

Zimmermann, Robert, "Zur Reform der Aesthetik als exacter Wissenschaft," [On the Reform of Aesthetics as an Exact Science] 309–360 in *Zeitschrift für exakte Philosophie* 2, 1862.

# INDEX

Adorno, Theodor 5, 6, 56–7, 103,
    128–9, 132–3, 134–9, 144, 145,
    152, 153
adventure 40–2
aesthetic education 24, 41
aesthetic experience: establishing
    existence of 157–8; as experience
    of self 14, 90; luxury as special form
    of 5–7, 63, 64, 81, 82, 85, 87,
    90–4, 116; luxury as defiant form
    of 115; operational orientation of
    87–9; perception and possession as
    forms of 7, 91, 92–7, 105–6;
    philosophy of 55; previous
    reflection required for 146–7,
    148–9, 150; self-referential quality
    of 14, 28, 34, 35, 38, 47, 88,
    89–90; sensual enjoyment different
    from 137, 146; sports and
    43, 116–17
aesthetic judgment 72, 88, 152
aesthetics of reception see reception
    aesthetics
aestheticism 151–2
akrasia 108
anthropology vii, 6, 7, 15,
    65–6
anti-grave 142
anxiety 38

apology see luxury, apology for
Aristotle 18–19
art 6, 45–7, 70, 86–7, 102, 104–5,
    106–7, 129, 134–40
art history 43–6, 112

Balzac, Honoré de 142
Baudrillart, Henri 53
beauty 4, 55, 86–7, 116, 118, 146–8,
    151–2, 153–4, 155, 157, 158
Benjamin, Walter 101–2
Bergengruen, Maximilian 2
Bernini 43–4, 47
Bildungsbürgertum (educated middle
    classes or intellectuals) 6, 102
boredom 43
Bourdieu, Pierre 61, 127
Brock, Bazon 132, 133

comfort 59–60, 137, 156
connoisseurship 149–50, 154
criticism see luxury, criticism of

Dadaism 112
Darwin, Charles 127
defiance 107–10
Descartes, René 22, 25, 42
Diogenes 122
DIY (do it yourself) 155–6

**170** Index

Donatello 43
drugs 40, 41–42

education vii, 102–3, 104, 129, 133
elegance 140–5
Enzensberger, Hans Magnus 123
elegance *see* luxury and elegance
existentialism 68, 115

feeling of life *see* Lebensgefühl
Fogg, Phileas 143–4
form of life 66, 71
freedom 7, 20, 35, 39, 68, 103, 111,
  113–14, 115, 125, 132–3
Fromm, Eric 96

Gehlen, Arnold 123
Geiger, Moritz 104
Goethe, Johann Wolfgang
  von 26
Goodman, Nelson 86
Görland, Albert 56–7
Gumbrecht, Ulrich 43, 116–17

health 74–6, 82–3, 149
Hegel, Georg Wilhelm 26,
  111–12
Heidegger, Martin 24, 29, 30, 31, 33,
  35, 36–9, 42, 46, 48, 63
*homo ludens* 15
Hornby, Nick 100
Hume, David 1
Husserl 17, 24, 30

image object 141–2
intellectuals *see* Bildungsbürgertum
interpretationism 77–81

Jaeggi, Rachel 66
Jaspers, Karl 38–9, 40
judgment and estimation 72–8,
  146–150, 152, 154, 157
Jung, Matthias 29
Jünger, Ernst 40–2, 47, 48, 63

Kant, Immanuel 4, 6, 7, 23, 34–5, 42,
  55, 60–1, 71–2, 73, 86, 88, 90, 94,
  95, 97, 104, 105, 118–20, 144,
  145–7, 151–2, 157
kitsch 55
Kleist, Heinrich von 142
Körner, Gottfried 23
Krockow, Christian Graf von 121
Krünitz, Johann Georg 57

Laocoön (sculpture group) 26, 28
Lazlo, Carl 113–14, 131
*Lebensgefühl* (feeling of life) 7, 19, 20,
  90, 107
Lessing, Gotthold Ephraim 25,
  27–8, 45
luxury: apology for 2–4; lack of
  consensus about 2–3; criticism of
  2–4, 103–7, 116–17; definition of
  (standard) 2, 58–9, 61; description
  of as classic phenomenological task 5;
  impossibility of buying 147;
  intentional as distinct from
  extensional understanding of 54,
  55, 112–13, 115; irreducibility of
  54; judgment of 7, 68, 69–77;
  judgment versus estimation of ;
  literature concerning viii; opaque
  as distinct from transparent 120;
  phenomenology of 4, 6, 13, 63, 91,
  113, 158; philosophical disinterest
  in 1–2, 56, 106; rarity and 123–4,
  156; in a tradition 8

Mandeville, Bernard 2
Marx, Karl 126, 128, 129
Merleau-Ponty 23, 30
Michelangelo 43, 44–5
Mühlmann, Horst 59–60

Nagel, Thomas 17
Nietzsche, Friedrich 65, 142
nonpurposeful *see* unpurposeful and
  nonpurposeful
Novalis 104

## Index 171

ostentation 55, 59, 61–4, 128–9, 133, 135

Pfänder, Alexander 30
phenomenology 6, 13, 14, 22–3, 24, 30–1, 63, 80, 91, 112, 158
play: anthropological function of 25, 27–8, 34; as diagnosis of Schiller's time 47; in everyday speech 39; games and 35; Heidegger's substitution of *anxiety* for 36–7; as intentionally different from luxury 115; Jaspers' *border situations* in place of 39; Jünger's *adventure* in place of 40–3; luxury as substitution for 13; as means of self-experience 23, 24–5, 28, 34, 112; as pregnant moment 27–8, 33, 112; Schiller's special concept of 13–22, 23, 24–5
possession: aesthetic of viii, 102, 106, 147; goal-oriented versus operationally-oriented 99; as intentional relationship 93; versus ownership 7, 93–5, 105; possessor's interest in 97–8; suitability to phenomenological investigation 95
pregnant moment 25–7; anthropologically significant 28, 33, 34, 35, 36, 38, 40–2, 43, 47, 48, 63, 90, 109, 115, 116, 158; existence of 33–4; Schiller's moment of play as 28, 35, 41
prestige 125, 128
property 93–5, 105, 106, 114, 155
*protreptikos* (protreptic writing) 23, 42
purpose without purposefulness 117–19, 138, 145, 149, 151, 158

Raphael 45
reception aesthetics 6, 25, 87, 91, 116
Rousseau, Jean-Jacques 2, 23, 77, 103

Sartre, Jean-Paul 30, 68, 115
Scheler, Max 22
Schiller, Friedrich 8, 13–22, 14–15, 20, 23, 25, 27–8, 33, 34, 35–6, 39, 41, 43, 47, 48, 109, 116
Schlegel, Friedrich von 46
Schwitters, Kurt 112–13
Seel, Martin 87, 89, 92
self-experience 7, 16–18, 19–21, 28, 33, 89–90, 149; inaccessibility to others 158; luxury as means of 111; pregnant moments of 25, 34, 41; as projection 146–7; *see also* aesthetic experience
*slavery of purposes* (Adorno) 144–5
Sloterdijk, Peter 109
Sombart, Werner 2, 57, 65, 69
Sommer, Manfred 30
sports 43, 116–17

tourbillon 150, 153
transgression 121
Turner, William 113

Ullrich, Wolfgang 62, 96, 102, 104, 106–7
unpurposeful and nonpurposeful 117–20, 136, 138, 149
Urwick, Edward John 67–8

Valéry, Paul 142–3, 144
Veblen, Thorstein 5, 103, 126, 127–9, 132, 133, 134–5
Verne, Jules 143, 144

war 40–1
Warhol, Andy 86
Weber, Max 121, 125, 126, 128, 149
Weder, Christine 2

Zimmermann, Robert 147

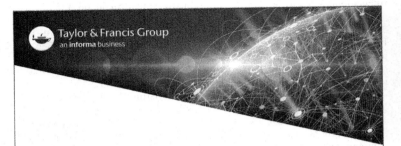